Straight to the Pointlessness

Straight to the Pointlessness

*A Christian account of
life and the universe*

Mark Hart

continuum

Published by the Continuum International Publishing Group
The Tower Building, 11 York Road, London SE1 7NX
80 Maiden Lane, Suite 704, New York NY 10038

www.continuumbooks.com

First published 2011

British Library Cataloguing-in-Publication Data
A catalogue record for this book is available from the British Library.

ISBN 978–1–4411–6396–7

Designed and typeset by Kenneth Burnley, Wirral, Cheshire
Printed and bound in Great Britain by the MPG Books Group

Contents

For the people of Plemstall and Guilden Sutton

Introduction

The title is quite appropriate, someone may say. Just what is the point of yet another book about Christianity? After nearly two thousand years of writing, is there really a need for anything new?

Perhaps the subtitle is a response. This is an account of life and the universe, and surely no one can claim that the last word has been said on that subject. It is true that I am giving a presentation of Christian faith, but as a way of interpreting ordinary life as valued by people today and the universe as understood by modern science.

The world is ill-served by the growing poles of strident atheism and religious fundamentalism. The one rightly aims to uphold the value of life and the benefit of rational enquiry into the universe, but denies any fruitfulness in the search for a deeper interpretation, for a source of that value and rationality which lies beyond ourselves. The other rightly admits the ultimate questions, but imposes with absolute certainty an answer which often cuts across both ordinary values and the results of rational enquiry.

Unfortunately, many identify Christianity with the latter, and this is only encouraged by both the beliefs of some parts of the Church and the excessive claims sometimes made for science. So it is often thought that to become a Christian it is necessary to close your mind to parts of the world. Science seems to offer a contradictory explanation, discrediting miracles. Moral thinking questions many of the ways in which God acts in the Bible. Other religions question the uniqueness of Christ. Historical research questions the reliability of the Bible. The Church's trustworthiness is questioned by its repeated failures through history.

All this modern awareness poses a serious challenge when the gospel of Jesus Christ itself is meant to be good news; that is, something which is *good*, concurring with our most deeply held values, and something which is *news*, important testimony in history to be welcomed and explored, demanding the attention of any honest, rational person who is open to truth. The last way in which the Church should react in the face of such questions is to deny the truth that can be found in the wider world. Nor should its engagement be merely defensive. According to the Christian faith, there is no truth that is not part of God's truth, and the Church must be open to truth without prejudice.

The aim of this book is therefore to show that by holding onto the ordinary values of life, and the thirst for rational enquiry, with an openness to discover a deeper interpretation and source of our being, we may come to see how the Christian faith can make sense as good news today; indeed, we may see that it is only in this way that Christian faith came into being in the first place.

The argument is apologetic to the extent that it anticipates and responds to the challenges of the modern world, but it is certainly not an attempt to establish the certainty of the faith by reason. To think that such an intellectual feat may be possible would contradict the central theme of this book, that life is a gift.

We did not create ourselves. We do not flourish as human beings simply by individual effort. Our fulfilment is only made possible with others, by giving and receiving. Such is God's life, and the life in which we are called to share. And if, in this way, gift is the ultimate truth, then it cannot be a truth which we may produce for ourselves by sheer reason. It can only be received as a gift, for otherwise we would be saying that the deepest truth is not gift but raw human intellect. The *fundamental* value in our lives would not lie in the world which our reason seeks to grasp – the love, joy, goodness and beauty which we experience – but in human reason itself. Of course, this is not an excuse to go against reason. On the contrary, I will argue that faith in God is continuous with that giving of ourselves which is necessary in order that our reason may ever be engaged with the world at all.

This book is a Christian account of the world which may provide food for thought and fresh insights for anyone interested in the faith. I have been concerned to respond to the objections of people who cannot understand how it is intellectually possible to be a Christian today. I also have in mind Christian readers who may be unsettled by modern objections to the faith, or who may never have faced up to them.

Not that the argument is structured around these challenges, which are discussed more incidentally in the context of building towards a coherent Christian understanding of life. This is, above all, an attempt to show how the elements of the Christian faith fit together, and thereby make sense of life and the universe as a whole. To do this it is necessary to think quite deeply, as well as broadly, which may seem impossible in such a short space. The result is necessarily condensed and sketchy. There is barely a paragraph which will not, for someone, cry out for clarification or qualification – or contradiction! However, the point is not to be exhaustive or conclusive, but to open windows onto new ways of thinking for many readers.

The more one moves from a statement of faith to an explanation, the more one is in territory where Christians disagree. In places I have acknowledged this, but I have not wanted to clutter or enlarge the text with constant reference to other viewpoints. It should be taken for granted that this is *an* account. Having said that, while it is not free of my idiosyncrasies, my intention has been that it should be rooted in Scripture, the Creeds, and the wider tradition of the Church. Furthermore, it is largely a collection of valued insights gleaned from many other writers. Foremost among these is Archbishop Rowan Williams, who has thrown open many windows for me. This is evident from the endnotes, but anyone acquainted with his work will notice it more generally. The book is not a summary of his thinking, but he deserves more credit for anything it contains of value than the endnotes provide.

Three months of sabbatical leave after Easter 2009 gave me the opportunity to write, for which I am very grateful to the Diocese of Chester and to the good people of the parishes of Plemstall and Guilden Sutton, where I serve, who took on extra responsibility. I am also most indebted and thankful to the following, who gave of their time to read an early draft: Peter Forster (Bishop of Chester), Keith Sinclair (Bishop of Birkenhead), David Clough (University of Chester), Denise Campbell, Bridget Earlam, Pauline Holgate, Peter Reid and John Scrivener (parishioners of Plemstall or Guilden Sutton). Together they provided an invaluable source of comment, correction, challenge and encouragement. It has also been a joy to work with Caroline Chartres as editor and I am grateful for her constant enthusiasm.

Finally, I could not have written this without the love and support of my family, through whom, above all, I know life to be a gift.

1 Straight to the Pointlessness

Everyone believes in freedom, but there are many distorted ideas about what it means and how it should be achieved. Religion is one of them, some would say. Not only may the truth of its beliefs be challenged (and we will later come to the question of how we can *know* anything of God), but the life it offers can sound limiting, not expanding. The very notion of God as a 'supreme being' highlights the problem for modern ears. If God matters above all else then our own well-being and that of the environment must be secondary.

Such concern is only encouraged by those who present God as an object of purpose in an otherwise aimless existence. One of the most popular Christian books written in recent times, *The Purpose Driven Life*, begins with this sentence, standing as a paragraph in itself: 'It's not about you.' Everything exists for the benefit of God, we are told, who has emotions which must be served by our pleasing behaviour.[1]

This is open to serious criticism for two reasons. First, because it devalues the world. It may be agreed that certain ways of life lack any goal. It would be a vicious circle if I both worked in order to provide for leisure and relaxed in order to be refreshed for work. However, the way out is not to find some ultimate end beyond either activity, but to make one, or better, each one, to be an end in itself.

Some actions are clearly not ends in themselves. When I post a letter it is with the purpose that someone will receive it. But what we value most in life we value for its own sake. At their highest, conversation, friendship, music, sport, art and feasting do not need to be useful towards some other objective. Someone may say that we engage in such activity for the *purpose* of achieving happiness, joy, delight or love. However, we should be careful not to say that these abstracted goods are the real ends of life. They are ways of describing life at its best, but it is life itself that is its own end, not the maximization of an abstract quality as if it were a separate entity. The best way to kill a conversation is for attention to be focused on the level of joy in the conversation rather than on each other.

If life seems aimless, and we cannot find joy in ordinary things, then the solution is not to introduce God as an alternative end. Friends who discover that my real delight lies not in their company, but in how the exercise functions for God, may rightly feel used.

The second criticism follows, for it is now clear that on this account God is in competition with everything else in the world to be the object of our lives. This is inevitable if it is asserted that we exist for God's *benefit*. Paradoxically, the pious intention of attributing all our purpose to be ultimately *for God* actually reduces God to be the same kind of being as us, only bigger and more powerful, trumping all other claims on our lives. Not only is the world devalued, so also is God. The modern distaste for a 'supreme being' is healthy, for 'supreme' merely places God at one end of the *same* scale.

This is at odds with the classical conception of God in Christian tradition, and I say that lest it is thought that I am conveniently revising the faith to be more palatable for today. Augustine was clear in his *Confessions*: 'It is from the fullness of thy goodness that thy creation exists at all . . . even though it can profit thee nothing.'[2]

God's being, life and fulfilment do not depend on anything but God. To speak of God's pleasure in creation cannot mean that it is of benefit to him. Creation does not add anything to God himself.

Why then did God create the world if it is fundamentally useless? Some analogy can be found in the experience of our lives already considered. The greatest value is found at those points where the action is not driven by purpose, necessity or usefulness, but is an end in itself. The world is characterized by excess or overflow beyond function. Or so it should be. The reason why God's action in creation can seem radically strange is because it cuts across much of the way we are disposed and pressurized to live. The more education is designed to make productive workers for society, the less children will find joy in learning for its own sake. The more sport is driven by financial gain, the less appropriate becomes the term *player*. And as the focus of any business is tightened by goals and plans, the less genuine and more calculated become even simple good manners.

It is obviously the case that functional activity is essential to our life, but function is not what life is about. The Sabbath of the Jewish tradition is unique among ancient religions in forbidding work. The Chief Rabbi, Jonathan Sacks, says, 'It was and is the one day in seven in which we live out all those values which are in danger of being obscured in the daily rush of events; the day in which we stop making a living and learn instead simply how to live.'[3]

This useless excess is written into the creation story at the beginning of the Bible, and the same theme appears throughout Scripture in the recurring vision of the end of all things as a feast of rich food and fine wine.

Eating is a most basic and necessary activity of life, yet in all cultures it has never been merely about survival or providing energy for work. Eating at its best is life at its best, with the food, company and environment all being sources of delight in themselves. Here is one small example of the kind of excess that can accompany a meal. A large team of us were eating in a restaurant at the end of a week of work together. The service was particularly good, to the point that it enhanced the enjoyment of the meal, going beyond the call of duty and performed with genuine pleasure. At the end the money was collected and each gave their part. The total was significantly more than necessary, including a very generous tip, or *gratuity*, which was received with joy, surprise and an appreciative response concerning the happy atmosphere of the occasion. There was no sense that the service was calculated to elicit the gratuity, nor that the gratuity was actually not a gratuity but buying some future favour.

An accurate but difficult word to describe everything about such a feast is 'gratuitous'. The reason it is difficult is that we almost never hear it used for anything other than violence, insults or pornography. I here want to reclaim the word since it helpfully combines the meanings of free, given, unnecessary and purposeless. It is a good word which can describe both life at its best and God's creation of the universe. The right sort of gratuitousness is what makes the world go round, in every sense.

God freely gives us life. He doesn't need to and he gets nothing from it for himself. He hasn't made us to be useful for his own needs nor for any other high purpose beyond the universe. Much as we may like to justify our existence, or achieve something which establishes our right to live, we cannot do so and need not do so.

The world is gratuitous because God's own life is gratuitous. Christian belief is not in a God who is an isolated individual, but in a unity who is also Father, Son and Holy Spirit; one God in whom there is self-giving and receiving. This is God's life of self-giving for God's sake, which is not made necessary by anything beyond God. By this interdependence God *is*, but God's life is not exhausted by what is necessary to *be*, to survive, just as ours is not. There is excess in God himself, displayed to us in the fact that God is a creator of that which is not God.

Creation comes from the overflow of who God is. It does not make God who he is or give him purpose. The world is not God, but it is God's will that it should share God's kind of life. That is what is meant when it is said that the world exists *for God*, or for his pleasure or glory. It is not to give life a purpose, a work which makes us useful for God himself. To suggest that would be to imply that we earn our right to exist. It would make God somehow dependent on us. It would remove any foundation for the gratuitous. It would open the possibility of any part of the world being claimed by me as justified only by being *useful* to me.

God is present to the world, not as the centre of attention, not as the one whom it is all about, but as the ground of its freedom to be itself by sharing in the delight and joy of his kind of life. The world exists for its own sake, and to live for God's glory means to recognize that creatures and creative activity are ends in themselves. Everything and everyone we encounter becomes a gift, but nothing and no one exists only for my benefit. No one is ever simply a means to an end. It is in this excess that joy lies, and life is a treadmill if each step is simply the way to achieve the next. If the point of a holiday is only to be refreshed for more toil, then we miss the pointlessness.

It is true that in order to live in this world we need each other, but we should not find our meaning in being needed, just as we should not find the meaning of others in our need of them. There is delight in such giving and receiving precisely because the interdependence does not exhaust the significance. The good of life is found in this gratuitous and pointless overflow beyond function. This is not to deny the sometimes difficult task we face of working out the response we should be to the world in the way we live, our 'calling' if you like, but that is never about finding a justification for ourselves.

It matters that we have a part, that we contribute to the life of the whole and in return receive life ourselves. In that sense we have a use. I am not suggesting that someone who has lost a 'sense of purpose' in life should simply be told not to care. But such a person is yearning not so much to be a tool or an instrument, but to be a player, and the part played need not be productive in the narrowly economic sense. If we ask what is the ultimate point of the life we create together, the answer must be that there isn't one, or that this life is its own point. And that is not a disappointment – it is our freedom. It is God's freedom, shared with us. There may be endless depths of love, joy and beauty to discover as God's life and glory is made present, and the pursuit of that may be described as a purpose, but it is never a burdensome task for the benefit of anything beyond itself. Why should we wish life to be essentially onerous? It is true nevertheless that life is not frivolous or trivial, and it can only be by a costly, sometimes painful process that we learn the necessary self-denial which does not *use* others as a means to an end. But the ultimate glory is that none of us is so used. We become free at the point of uselessness.

At the end of his short book *The Meaning of Life*, the literary critic Terry Eagleton, not writing from any particular faith perspective, proposes the improvisation of a jazz group as an image of life at its best:

> The complex harmony they fashion comes not from playing from a collective score, but from the free musical expression of each member acting as the basis for the free expression of the others. As each player grows more musically eloquent, the others draw inspiration from this and are spurred to greater heights . . . There is self-realization, but only through a loss of self in the music as a whole. There is achievement, but it is not a question of self-aggrandizing success . . . There is pleasure . . . happiness . . .
>
> . . . What we need is a form of life which is completely pointless, just as the jazz performance is pointless. Rather than serve some utilitarian purpose or earnest metaphysical end, it is a delight in itself. It needs no justification beyond its own existence.
>
> In this sense, the meaning of life is interestingly close to meaninglessness. Religious believers who find this version of the meaning of life a little too laid-back for comfort should remind themselves that God, too, is his own end, ground, origin, reason, and self-delight, and that only by living this way can human beings be said to share in his life.[4]

This is not far from the kingdom of God, revealed through Jesus Christ, who overturned all notions of what God's rule may be about. The picture of God and creation which I have given above stands in contrast to the natural way in which many tend to think. God is not at the other end of the same scale, or even off the scale. As the theologian David Burrell put it, this misconceives God to be 'the biggest thing around'. But God is neither 'big' in the sense of 'like us but larger', nor a 'thing' in the sense of an object which we can identify. He is not a part of creation, but neither is he alongside all the things of creation in competition for our attention.

God is in the depth as the foundation of creation, the ground up-holding all that exists, but not imposing his presence on it. God allows creation to exist for its own sake and to have its own integrity. God's act of creation is a self-renunciation, a letting be. It is a rule of service, where God provides all that is necessary for his life to be shared, but the essence of that life is self-denial.

That is why we live in a world where you can be forgiven for doubting that God even exists. For many today it is possible to find value in life and make sense of things without reference to God. This does of course leave a serious question about the origin of our values, among other things. I suggest that such a way of life is something like when a cartoon character goes over the edge of the cliff and is suspended in mid-air, before plunging into free-fall on recognizing that there is nothing to sustain. There is an exhilarating illusion of 'freedom' that relies on pre-tending that there is still some ground for value. But such lives should certainly not be dismissed as 'empty', as if God exists to fill a need in us; or 'aimless', as if we exist to fill a need in God.

A particularly unhelpful way to encourage faith in God is to insist that, because he is the all-powerful creator, the supreme being, he is more important than all the ordinary activities of life. The acknowledge-ment of God – meaning religious activity – should obviously take priority because he is number one, it is suggested. Such thinking colludes with the view that life is essentially a competition where each is seeking to establish and protect a domain which is under one's control. Religion is always at risk of becoming a bid for the very power which it is its purpose to dispossess. The same religion which warns of the idolatry inherent in the pursuit of all manner of inordinate desires can create a demanding God who is just another idol. But an idol is not something which displaces God, as if God is an imposing presence whose territory can be infringed. An idol is rather anything which removes the freedom underwritten by God that nothing should be such a totalitarian presence, not even God himself; the freedom which insists that no creature should ever be told 'It's not about you.'

Salvation *may* be described as God in his power coming to rescue the world in its weakness, but the deepest understanding of the gospel of Jesus Christ is of God in his weakness rescuing the world from its power. In all of creation and salvation, God goes beyond his self in order to save us from holding on to our selves. God does nothing but divest to save us from doing nothing but invest. He delivers us from the tyranny of purpose, where every action is performed for some calculated advantage, a tyranny which promises the world yet eats the soul.

When true to its source, the Church is therefore unconcerned with gaining or retaining territory, but with giving and living out such freedom. It came into being as the anticipation of a new creation where everything is free and nothing is exploited for a purpose; where joy flows from the discovery of how each can be a useless gift to the other; where the worship of God is not about losing freedom through serving his needs, but purposeless delight and wonder in response to the vision of his glory. It goes without saying that the Church often appears otherwise, but I hope to show that this is where its faith is rooted.

2 Intimations of God

It may be surprising to hear it said that according to the Christian faith everything is gratuitous, that life is given for no ultimate purpose. Does that mean there is no practical difference between Christianity and atheism? Not at all. The difference is this: if I do not believe in a Giver, how can I see everything as given and gratuitous?

Without God there is no truth outside of myself which answers the question of the meaning of life, not even a truth which says everything is purposeless. I can choose to live unselfishly and respectful of the integrity of others, but I can also choose to live as if things and people exist only for my benefit, without contradiction of any truth I know about the universe. Nothing is sacred; nothing bears limits on how it may be used.

Everything becomes a matter of taste. A serial killer's decision at breakfast concerning the identity of that day's victim becomes no different in kind from a decision to have marmalade on his toast. In neither case is there an external, objective reason to guide. The fact that most people disapprove of the former is of no help. It makes his taste unusual, about as unusual as a choice to have marmalade on both sides of his toast, but it makes it no more objectively wrong. Yet we call one of these actions inhuman, and the other merely eccentric.

In response to this it is often claimed that God does not give any more sure a ground for morality. For consider the following question, posed in its original form by Plato. Is what is good commanded by God because it is good, or is it good because it is commanded by God? This is a dilemma, for if the former is true, goodness is prior to God and cannot therefore be grounded in him. If the latter is true, then what is good is arbitrary: if God declares murder to be good, then it is good.

This is an important and illuminating argument, but the fallacy, in the opinion of many, is the assumption that God and goodness can be separated in this way such that the two horns of the dilemma are the only options. As we have seen, the life we are called to is to be understood primarily as God's life, not as obedience to a set of commands in isolation.

To handle God and goodness in this logical way has the same feel about it as doing arithmetic with infinity as if it can be handled like any other number. This leads to contradiction. Infinity plus one must still equal infinity, since there is nothing greater than infinity. But that must imply that one equals zero. However, we don't conclude that the concept of infinity is invalidated. Rather, we realize that it must be handled with care.

As we have seen, a common mistake is to regard God as another object alongside everything else that exists. From this assumption it is possible to derive objections to his existence, for as the unexplained gaps in the world have closed, so the space for such a God has diminished. We shall come later to the reason why we may trust that God is not like this, and why he therefore cannot be 'handled' at all by any thinking that presumes to encompass him.

So I am not persuaded by the 'dilemma' and find myself unable to let go of the foundational assumption that the torture of a child, for example, is wrong, meaning not merely that I don't like it, or that it does nothing for me, but that there is a truth about the child which is prior to any of my appetites and desires, a sacredness which is grounded in its relationship to God.

I am not denying that morals can be constructed without God, nor am I claiming that atheists cannot be as good-living as Christians. In practice, atheists take it as *given* that human life should be valued, for example, and hold firmly to such a principle. But 'given' can never mean more than 'given by human minds'. Atheists cut off any exploration into the possibility of truth intrinsic to what we value which may account for that value which our minds give. When the apple fell on Isaac Newton's head, he was not content to rest with the fact that a sensation was present within him. He looked beyond himself in faith that he may find some understanding. To seek for God is no different.

I do not offer this as conclusive proof for the existence of God. I am also conscious of the question for Christianity of the existence of evil and suffering. But leaving the 'problem of evil' aside for the moment, I suggest that without God there remains a 'problem of good'.

Why then have atheism and agnosticism increased in recent times, at least in the more developed nations? Is it because of increased suffering? Apparently not, for generally speaking atheism is less common among the poorest in the world and more common among the comfortable.

In wealthier countries a higher level of education and a greater enjoyment of the fruits of technological innovation have given rise to a wider appreciation of the explanatory power of science. Alongside this is the popular perception, not without some justification, that Christianity has hindered the progress of science. There is a strong counter-argument to be made, but that debate is not my purpose here.

Some would argue that Christianity is in retreat because it is simply no longer needed. From primitive times when the capricious wills of a pantheon of gods were thought to determine the activity of all the different elements of the world, humanity has grown to understand that *will* has nothing to do with it. If everything just follows laws of nature, then each event can be explained by the previous state of affairs, without the need to introduce any external agent.

In response, it must first be said that it cannot be shown using science itself that everything is reducible to physical scientific laws. Such a claim conflicts with faith in God, but since it is not scientific it does not bring *science* into conflict with faith. It is a belief, like belief in God, in a way, in that it cannot be based on unquestionable rational argument. It would only be purely rational if science had so progressed that it was clear to everyone that there was no question left in the universe which science could not answer.

Yet we have already met one: from whence come the good and the sacred? It has been shown that without God we are left effectively denying that these really exist. Science is completely neutral with regard to value. It doesn't know the language.

Physical science studies the world through a particular filter, so it does not see the whole world. A clue to this is the impersonal style of report writing which students are taught to use in their very first classes. 'You' and 'I' are taken out of it, for all that matters is what is objective and measurable.[1]

Science works with such properties as mass, distance, time and charge. For a given body under investigation only a certain range of qualities can be objectively observed. It is a huge leap to claim that these qualities are the only qualities and tell the whole truth.

Consider this repeatable phenomenon. I come downstairs in the morning and open the study curtains. Occasionally the sunrise over Great Barrow catches my attention. In terms of purely physical properties it is no more remarkable than any other day. Just a different set of numbers, and one number is as unremarkable as another. But from me it draws out awe and wonder. Even if you wish to deny any deeper reality to the sunrise, you have to accept my testimony of a truth about me. A truth which science, I suggest, can never reach. Suppose I were wired up and scanned, and precise correlations between electrical and chemical brain activity and my experience were discovered, the awe and wonder itself would still not have been observed or explained. How may it ever be possible for physical science of the brain to explain conscious experience?

The philosopher David Chalmers called this the 'hard problem', and the name has stuck among consciousness researchers. To show why it is hard, consider what would be a comparatively trivial problem. I open the curtains and, instead of the sunrise, it is the car on the drive which draws my eye. Every so often, without any apparent force acting, it levitates, spins around in various directions, and then returns to its original place. In this case scientists have a phenomenon which can be precisely and independently observed and measured, and they can camp outside with their instruments ready for the next movement. It may require the revision of a few theories, but it is conceivably explicable by physical laws.

By contrast, no one has a clue how to even begin to explain consciousness with physics, for experience itself cannot be described in the language of physics. So, as with the question of goodness, some deny any reality to consciousness. It is argued that once we can explain all the easy parts about our brains and behaviour, consciousness will be revealed to have been an illusion. I have tried, but fail to see how this can make sense as a possibility. It should give pause to us that to maintain the exhaustive scope of science it is again necessary to deny what seems fundamental.

Personal, subjective experience is a reality and offers another reason to believe that there is more truth to the universe than physical science can ever tell. For many, this naturally leads to the thought that the personal is not merely something which has emerged late in the life of the universe, but which lies at the origin of all things.

It does not follow that we must consider ourselves to have a dual nature, comprising material bodies and a detachable, immaterial 'soul'. It rather suggests that there is more to matter than meets the scientists' instruments. And this is no denigration of science, which remains a glorious, creative and fruitful endeavour, even though it by no means offers an end to all our questioning.

It is telling that the most ardent atheists still want to speak passionately of their awe and wonder at the world. I would interpret wonder as a recognition of the excess beyond the functional which may be found in creation, which I described earlier. It is to perceive a sunrise or a piece of music to have intrinsic worth, to be an end in itself. But it is impossible for the person who believes that everything is reducible to science to attribute such value objectively. So, while I have argued that it is very difficult to imagine how physical science could get a handle on wonder, if we suppose it did, what would that mean? Once the network of causes was unravelled and laid before us to explain our wonder, we would have to sigh, 'No wonder.'

Finally, there is the mother of all 'givens' to which science can barely respond. Of the primary values, 'beauty, truth and goodness', it is just about possible, as we have seen, for atheists to deny any objective reality to beauty and goodness, to deny that they are really 'given'. But there is one objective *truth* which cannot be denied: there is something and not nothing. Why is there anything at all? The sheer existence of ourselves and the wonderful world in which we live makes us ask where we came from. And if we accept (and this is quite a big 'if') that all the development of the universe from the Big Bang onwards has been without any divine guidance, we are left asking where those equally wonderful first conditions came from.

At whatever point we stop, we find contingency: What touch has brought this to be? We wonder where the universe came from, since it had a beginning. And we wonder why it is like it is, since we can easily imagine it being different. So we want to trace back, asking those questions, until we find something which didn't come from anywhere, because it is eternal and has no beginning, and which necessarily is what it is.

The God of the Christian faith satisfies these questions, so we don't have to ask 'Who made God?' God does not depend on anything other than himself for his existence. According to the Christian understanding of God, he is *necessary*, not contingent, for no reality is possible without him. We can suppose that the world never had bananas, but in distinction from all the objects we find in the world, a believer cannot suppose that we never had God. (Note that this does not contradict the gratuitous life of God described previously, for the point made there is that nothing *other* than God makes his life necessary.)

Is there an alternative answer? The most commonly held candidate is the multiverse hypothesis. It works something like this. When an individual wins the lottery there is great surprise because the probability of winning is so low. But no one is surprised that *someone* has won, because the number of players is very large. Imagine if this universe is not all there is, but there are actually many. Suppose that everything that could possibly exist does exist. Then there is no longer any surprise or contingency in our existence.

At first sight this seems quite neat, but there are significant problems. What is meant by 'everything that could possibly exist'? Does not this extravagance stand in some contrast to the normal scientific approach of adopting the simplest solution? Do we have to entertain the possibility of countless thoroughly evil worlds? And finally, the theory seems to eat itself, for we could reasonably suppose that God is one of the possibilities and then find that there is no need of the multiverse.[2]

I still do not claim to have offered anything like proof of the existence of God. Atheism, supported by science, does a service when it exposes the weakness of all attempts to provide evidence for God in the way evidence may be provided for the existence of an undetected elementary particle, for example – as a gap in the world needing an explanation. The more we realize that we do not find God by looking for where he may have imposed his presence, the better. The Church must live disarmed of clinching arguments and incontrovertible evidence, recognizing that this is how it must be if God's way is to serve the world's freedom.

The point of this chapter is rather that without God there remains a nagging concern, because we are left not with a gap *in* the world, but a gap *beneath* the world. The cost of reducing everything to be explained by science is that dignity, love and wonder, even the wonder of existence itself, are all deprived of any depth.

This has been a ground-clearing exercise to show that God cannot be comfortably dismissed. Few people are led all the way to faith by such arguments, but some are hindered by the lack of hearing them. Many simply conclude that they do not know, or even that no one can know with a practical certainty which allows commitment either way. With that there may still be a sense of frustration that if God really is such a giver, why has he not at least given unmistakable evidence of his existence? And if he is ultimately the giver of all things, including faith, how may it be received? It is to such questions that we now turn.

3 Faith and Reason

It is often thought that atheists have a claim to the rational high ground on the basis that they only accept truth which has been verified by reason and evidence. They do not rely on any additional leap, like faith.

This has a superficial appeal, but it first must be observed that without God, along with beauty and goodness, reason itself is also deprived of any depth. Just as I cannot lift myself up by my own bootstraps, so I cannot by my reason alone show why I should be reasonable, or why reason works in any practical sense. By its very nature atheism cuts itself off from the possibility of answers to such questions. It is therefore arguably less committed to reason because it disallows the possibility of a greater source of reason than our own minds. By contrast, if our reason is understood to be a *given* (rather than something which just happens to have appeared out of an irrational process) then it must be grounded in the Giver.

Furthermore, we all accept fundamental assumptions which we take on trust because without them we cannot live sensibly and rationally. I expect the world to behave with a basic regularity, even though there is no scientific or purely logical reason why gravity should still apply when I wake in the morning. I believe that things continue to exist even when I am not observing them. I regard other people whom I meet as conscious beings, even though strictly speaking I have no access to verification. Personal relationships can never be based purely on reason, yet we regard the knowledge of people as something rather more precious than the knowledge of facts. When two people fall in love, while it may sometimes be against all common sense to allow it to happen, it certainly need not be. Something can happen which is not produced simply by reason but which nevertheless does not go against reason. Similarly, when I see the sunrise or listen to Mozart, or when an artist responds to life by creating poetry or music, or when a student's breath is taken away by Einstein's theories of relativity – in all this something more than reason is involved.

Reason is that faculty by which we seek to grasp an object to understand how one part is related to another, or how a cause produces an effect. In order for this faculty to be active it is necessary that we first give ourselves to the object in the sense that we are engaged, not with ourselves and our needs and feelings, but with the other. Put like this, we see how faith must precede reason. If we do not first open ourselves to the possibility of discovery, and begin to search, trusting that there is something to be found at the end of the road, we will find nothing. Newton had to go beyond the feeling in his head and consider the apple.

All the above examples of 'something more than reason' are cases where that self-giving is happening, but the object is never fully grasped in a rational way. We give ourselves to the new day trusting that the world is still going round even though logic cannot tell us that it will. A couple may give themselves to each other for a lifetime knowing that rationally they will never exhaust all there is to know about each other. We are drawn out of ourselves to find beauty and wonder in an object but cannot fully analyze either by reason.

This is instructive because it demonstrates not that we sometimes live contrary to reason, but that we do not live only by reason. In fact, what we value most is that way of living where reason is engaged but conscious of its limits, aware that there is an excess beyond what we have grasped.

Faith in God is therefore continuous with the way we normally live. It is not a leap in the dark by contrast with the sure foundation of reason. It is to take the same kind of step that is necessary for reason to be actively engaged with the world. The difference lies in the kind of knowledge which can be attained, not in a fundamental difference of approach.

As I have already indicated, according to the classical understanding which I am presenting here, God is not an object, and cannot be located by us for investigation in the way we study a part of the universe. It is easy to say that God ought to intrude to provide unmistakable evidence that he is existent, personal and trustworthy, to allow us to build knowledge of him in the same way in which we come to understand the world. But that is to ask either for God not to be God, to be a part of the universe instead of its ground, or to ask for us not to be different from God, to be absorbed into him. What God has created is not God, and is created for its own freedom and integrity. The cost of this is that God is not necessarily obvious, as we have seen. He made us to be free, that we may by that freedom find him by finding each other. It is through our openness to the gift of the whole creation that we are pointed to God, for we may never directly apprehend him.

God is not just another *thing* to be discovered in the totality of all that exists. He is not a part of any total, not a member of any class, not an instance of any kind of being. If God is the creator of everything that is not God, then his being is fundamentally *other* than that of any part of creation. We are safer saying what God is not. We do need to describe God positively, but always aware that we are using analogy, never able to grasp him in our categories of thought. When we speak of God being 'in heaven', this helpfully recognizes that creation is not limited to the universe we see, and that God is not contained in this world. Yet it should not be understood to imply that God is contained in heaven either. It is better to take it to mean that he has his own space, or rather *is* his own space, for God has no body or location, his existence being dependent on nothing other than himself.

At its best, Christian thinking steers carefully between two pitfalls. In order to emphasize God's closeness, his immanence, it is tempting to identify God with the world as a part of creation – the way of pantheism. In order to emphasize God's power and transcendence it is tempting to conceive of God as a separate being outside the universe – the way of deism. But God is his own context and environment. He is neither the same as creation nor another thing like it.

So the way we must speak of God being present anywhere is as one who is present to all things as the context, ground and cause of their being. God neither shares our environment nor is he contained in a different environment. He is the reality who underlies every element of creation, including space and time itself. We should not think of God's omnipresence as a diffusion throughout all *space*, for we then fall into the trap of making creation the context for God. Neither should we imagine God to be in time in the way we are.

In this sense we may say both that we live in God, for whatever environment we are in has its context in God, and that God lives in us, for however deep we look inside ourselves, God is there as a greater depth. So Paul quotes to the Athenians one of their own poets: 'In him we live and move and have our being' (Acts 17.28). And Augustine, at the end of all his searching, acknowledges 'thou wert within'.[1]

Because nothing can contain God, he transcends this universe, but by the same freedom he is therefore able to be 'more intimate to us than we are to ourselves'.[2]

Imagine you are a two-dimensional being living in a two-dimensional world something like a piece of paper. If another piece of paper is placed beneath, then it is closer to every part of you than anything else in your world, while at the same time it is not contained in your world. We live in three dimensions, or four if we include time. We may think of God as wrapped around every part of us, within and without, including our past and our future, yet at the same time not being contained in our world. Of course, this analogy fails at the point where it suggests that God is another thing like the world, but it does the limited job of showing how immanence and transcendence can be held together. A more practical way is simply to pray as Jesus taught us, saying, 'Our *Father* who art in *heaven.*'

So while our reaching out for God is of a kind with every level of searching to make sense of the world, God can never yield to our analysis in the same way as matter. Because of his transcendence, God remains beyond our grasp, and because of his immanence, we can never step back to place him at arm's length for inspection. It is impossible for us ever to apprehend God by our science and philosophy, either to prove his existence or to delineate his character, for he is the ground of all our thinking. How could we ever, by our thinking, verify the ground by which we can think at all? On what other ground could we stand? The ultimate truth about ourselves can never be something which we produce for ourselves. It can only be received as a gift.

This requires a measure of openness. We make a distinction between knowing someone and knowing *of* someone. To know personally is to be in a relationship in which there is two-way communication: word and response, each recognizing the other as personal. Such knowledge cannot be obtained without a prior openness to the other as a person. It means recognizing that there is always more to another human being than a piece of matter to be analyzed. We cannot ever really 'see through' a person or 'get to the bottom' of their actions. It is through someone's behaviour towards us that we come to know them, but without that person ever becoming merely an object to us. Similarly, we only know God through his actions, with the difference that God is never an object to be analyzed. For a human being there is an excess beyond being an object, but God is nothing but excess.

We have a choice to make about each human being with whom we come into contact. We may recognize a *person* and sense a call upon ourselves, or we may regard the encounter as merely a means to an end. We all know when we have experienced the latter, whether in a shop, on the telephone, or in circumstances more significant. And if we are honest, we know when we have been short or inattentive. It is no accident that a bad-mannered person is described as 'ignorant', for there is a lack of *knowledge*, of personal knowledge. Of course, the openness we owe is not necessarily easy, because it always involves trust. By making myself available to another I am open to receive uncomfortable truth about myself. I also make myself vulnerable to any bad faith on their part. And the more we have experienced such treatment, the less inclined we may be to entrust ourselves.

Similarly, knowing God comes by entrusting ourselves. Just as I may regard another person's presence as *something* to calculate and reason my way through, rather than *someone* to whom I must give a faithful response, so I may live in the world as a whole that way. Alternatively, I may recognize the limits of calculation, weighing of evidence, and reason, and see the world and my own existence as spoken by God, to whom I must be a faithful response.

It is therefore clear that faith in God is never mere acknowledgement of his existence. 'I believe in God' is, from the beginning, an expression of trust and love – and good manners. It is to open ourselves to God, to be vulnerable to him. When a Christian speaks of 'knowing God' it should therefore never be a private claim (so infuriating to atheists and agnostics) to have direct, unmediated apprehension of naked deity (as if that is ever the way we know other humans as people). Nor is it measured by knowledge of the Bible or an ability to discourse theologically. It is an openness to the world as called into being by God's creative speech, and therefore an openness of ourselves to God's creative word to transform us; just as, in entering any faithful human relationship, we open ourselves to be changed by the words of another person.

For this reason, many Christians have described their experience of faith as an awareness of being known by God, more than of knowing God. And the greatest witness to the reality of faith is in transformed lives. The Bible is the witness of people who, having experienced such change, go on to trust him further and discover what must therefore be true about him. That is why it is written more as history than philosophy. The people of Israel looked back to the Exodus story of their deliverance from Egypt as a foundation of their faith. The first disciples of Jesus experienced his risen life before anything had been worked out about what it all meant. If we cannot apprehend God directly, then our knowledge of him is gained only from his acts, from the history of creation itself. Of course, this is not straightforward if creation has its own life and freedom, for God's own purpose and will cannot always be read directly off the surface. To do that would be to attribute all kinds of evil to God as well as good. That is why the community of faith has grown through experience of deliverance. If everything were random there would be nothing to draw us to trust in God. In giving this world its own integrity, God's creative action is a constant draw towards the freedom of his own life, and it is in the discernment of the signs of this that he can be known.

It is not possible to be a Christian without relying on the witness of others. Faith is nurtured in community – hardly surprising given that it is to do with an openness to creation as a gift. A cynic who dismisses all the testimony of others as 'man-made religion' and who engages on a private quest is likely to be disappointed. As Paul said, 'faith comes from what is heard' (Romans 10.17).

None of this is to say that faith should always come easily, nor is it by any means straightforwardly true that 'believers' are more open, trusting people by nature. Cynicism, bitterness and bigotry can keep people from faith, but they can also hold people in oppressive forms of faith. And it is possible to find the existence of God too easy to accept. A comfortable, self-satisfied, myopic tyrant may find belief in a certain kind of God rather natural, but it would hardly be to his credit as against someone traumatized by abuse who can barely trust another human, let alone God.

But it does in the end come down to our willingness to search and to be searched. I alone know the degree of honesty *I* bring, and even in that I can deceive myself. Believers may be accused of tipping the scales with wishful thinking, but there are also motives for not wanting God to exist. Christians above all should be open to the whole truth, including anything which makes faith more difficult. They should not be guided by any thoughts of a need to protect God, nor be closed to hearing the perspectives of people of other faiths and none.

Perhaps the most powerful witness of Christians has not been testimony to utter certainty, unclouded vision and undimmed hope, but the tenacity of faith through doubt, despair and protest, in the darkest experiences of life, to the point that all sense of God's presence may be gone, and wishful thinking hardly possible. Such was the way of Christ himself.

4 Growth of Faith

It should be clear that I am not claiming that the understanding of God which I am presenting here is derivable from first principles just by observation of nature and some philosophical thought. At the same time, since I have described the act of creation as God letting the world be itself, it is difficult to accept that he can simply step in and impose himself incontrovertibly. Knowledge of God, therefore, does not come easily, but by a gradual, repeating process whereby a little faith allows God to work towards salvation, and that experience of salvation leads to more faith and understanding. Of course, I will be claiming that the Bible leads us to faith and understanding, but we have the Bible by means of this process, not by an interruption of it. Similarly, we shall see Jesus as part of God's same way of working, and indeed the one through whom we understand that this is God's way of working.

The beginning of the Bible may lead us to think that from earliest times the people of Israel knew their God as the creator of the heavens and the earth, but this faith only developed after a long journey of deliverance. In order to appreciate this it is helpful to think through how Israel's experience may have formed their faith; to ask, given their starting point (very different from that of a person without faith now who has the benefit of a scientific understanding of the world, among other things) what reflection on that experience may lead to; to ask how it became possible to write the opening chapters of the book of Genesis, and more.

Imagine that you live thousands of years ago in a culture where each tribe has its own God. Your God is not at all like God as I have described him. He is very much contained in an environment and competing with others. For as long as anyone can remember, your small, weak tribe has been enslaved by an awesomely powerful people. Then one day, dramatically and miraculously, you are set free. It is a liberation which runs completely against the long-established order. It is something new and inexplicable. You thank your God, and enjoy your freedom. And you begin to think.

If my God has been able to overthrow such power, who may stand against him? Whatever we come against, we should be able to trust him. Indeed, no other god is his equal. Our God is so great that in comparison other gods are not gods. They are as powerless as a piece of stone or wood.

This means that our God is not just *our* God. He is effectively the God of all peoples, if they but knew it, which means that he isn't there just to serve our political ends. He isn't our God just for our sake. If he has delivered us, it cannot be so that we are free to oppress others. It may even be that our freedom is to be the means of bringing freedom to others.

But it doesn't stop there. If I can really trust, then nothing in heaven and earth is beyond his power, from the depths of the sea, to the sun and the stars. Everything is answerable to his command. I can go so far as to believe that he is the creator of everything that is not God; that everything was created from nothing, and the only reason it exists the way it does is because that is what God wants.

This tests my faith further. Have I been created because he needs me, or am I *really* free? If I can believe that God has made the world for its own sake, then I can go on to conclude that God is perfect in himself, needing nothing other than himself for that perfection. (Note that this is not to suggest that we can never fully trust other people who need us. Our need of each other is not something we have any choice about, so we may still be trustworthy. On the other hand, if God has *created* us because he needs us, then we are fundamentally instruments.)

It gets even more exhilarating. I have now come to see the whole world as called into being by God's word. Just as I recognize another human as a person to whose words and actions I must give a response, so I see all creation as God's act, which, like a word, calls forth from us a response.

Now I know just from looking at myself that our own words and actions don't always 'give much away', as we put it. We may not necessarily be deceitful, but we may be wary, recognizing a need to protect ourselves. There can be a gap between what we see and hear of another person, and what they really are.

However, if I can trust God, then, unlike us, he must show who he is. He is not acting deceitfully in order to use me, nor has he any reason to protect himself from me. This means that the very fact that God gives of himself at all in the act of creation suggests that 'giving of himself' is true of him apart from creation. God does not become a giver by creating, thereby increasing his glory; he creates because he is a giver.

Similarly, just as God receives a response through the act of creation which is the reflection of his glory, so response and reflection must be true of God in himself apart from creation. God does not become himself through creation; he reveals himself in creation.

So, by thinking through what it means to trust more, I have been led to believe that, in himself, God is both self-giver and given-self; one who speaks and the word who is spoken, revealing and reflecting back to the one who speaks.[1]

All this makes me hopeful about the future, believing that God really has created us for the kind of freedom where people live as gifts to each other. But a puzzle remains about how God may achieve this, and indeed about how he has delivered my tribe. On the one hand, my experience has taught me to trust God and to know him as one who speaks. By his word the world is formed, and by his word we must be guided. On the other hand, if the goal is freedom, how can this word ever compel without denying that goal? This cannot be a word which simply directs and controls. The world needs to hear the word in order to be set free, but it will only truly be open to hearing the word when it *has* been set free.

If all that I have said so far of God's relation to the world is all that can be said, then it seems we are locked out of freedom by a vicious circle. At the same time, I may have an uneasy feeling that God is locked into an 'unvicious circle'[2] by his life of mutual giving and receiving. In God, there is one who speaks, and one who reflects back, and each one exists wholly for the other. It seems like a mutual possession, where there is no love from the other which is for anyone other than me; where there is no giving of love to another whose life is not only for me. But that is just the kind of love which seems to be visible in the creation of the world. So I am led to think that the love in God himself must be a love which overflows to yet another in God, to break the 'unvicious circle'. And I am also led to think that there is a love from God which overflows into this world, to break the vicious circle.

Does that sound a plausible train of thought for someone living in the ancient world? The phrase 'wise after the event' may come to mind. The

Old Testament, of course, does not go all that way, but the possibility of being led towards the beginning of a Trinitarian understanding of God as three-in-one just by following your theological nose down a path of faith is significant, giving some confirmation of the process I have proposed, and demonstrating that in Israel the foundation was laid for what would later come through Christ.

What the Old Testament does tell is the story of a people who have known God's deliverance in the past and have therefore come to know God in a radically new way. The precise history of events and the development of thinking are not of immediate relevance here but, importantly, many of the above steps may be seen to have been made, as we see in the following brief summary.

The God of Israel is the one God, and idolatry is strictly forbidden. He is the creator of all things in heaven and on earth. (The creation of the stars, for example, bodies once thought to be deities, is mentioned as an aside in the first chapter of Genesis.) Israel are the people through whom all the nations of the earth will be blessed. God has created through his Word. He is one who speaks, and makes himself known through his acts, and calls for our response. A written law of history and command is therefore the appropriate expression of this, and to love and obey this law is to love and obey God himself.

Moreover, God is experienced as present and active in a different way: by his spirit, wind or breath (all from the same Hebrew word). This spirit hovers over the waters at the beginning of creation, even before the word is spoken, and is an agent in the whole of creation. The breath of God gives life to each human being. It was a wind which drove back the sea during the Exodus from Egypt. By his spirit God dwelt in the midst of them as a people. By the spirit coming upon them, individuals may be energized, encouraged, inspired and gifted for extraordinary works of prophecy, craftsmanship and leadership.

In particular, the spirit of the Lord 'came mightily' (1 Samuel 16.13) upon David when he was anointed king by Samuel. The throne of David was declared to be 'established for ever' (2 Samuel 7.16), and Israel, when later in exile, focused its hopes for future deliverance on the coming of an anointed one or Messiah (Hebrew for 'anointed') from the same 'stock of Jesse' (Isaiah 11.1). Concerning him, the Lord decrees, 'You are my son' (Psalm 2.7, cf. v. 2), and repeatedly the prophecy of Isaiah describes him as one on whom the spirit of the Lord will rest.

And what will characterize this new age? There will be a new spirit within, bringing life to the dead and transforming hearts of stone to hearts of flesh so that God's law may be kept. And the spirit will be poured out on the land and on all the people to make the desert a fruitful field, and to renew the vision and speech of all, from the youngest to the oldest.

The people of Israel clearly came to understand that God's word alone was not sufficient to explain either the extraordinary things they had seen and heard in the past, or the hope which they held for the future. He was not just present to them as one who speaks, he could also some-how be present among them and within them to bring new life.

A sceptic may not be convinced by the witness of ancient Israel alone, but we can certainly see that the unique development of their faith is consistent with the experience of salvation which their history claimed. They believed that the God who had delivered them from Egypt, and then from Babylon, held all creation in being by his word and spirit, and by the same word and spirit led them to freedom.

For Christians, all of what this chapter points to is fulfilled in Christ (the Greek for 'anointed'), who at his baptism was declared by God to be his Son, as the Holy Spirit descended upon him, and through whom we may now know God as one God, who is Father, Son and Holy Spirit. That whole story we will come to a little later. But next it is necessary to think more about the Spirit's work in creation. Isn't this a rather vague way to speak about God? Does it tell us anything new? Or does it just give a name to those parts of experience which we can't explain? And if the Spirit is so effective, why is there so much left to do?

5 God and Creation

Why did God not create a universe which was perfect from the start? One answer to this in the Christian tradition is that he did, but it all went wrong at the Fall when the first human beings disobeyed God. The price of freedom was the possibility that it may be abused. Because of sin, humanity and the world as a whole have become corrupted, and the Christian gospel is about how everything may be rescued and restored to a new creation.

The difficulty with this is that we now know, if we accept that life on earth has evolved over hundreds of millions of years, that before responsible humans existed there was disease, pain and death among animals. And nature's redness in tooth and claw hardly looks like mutual self-giving. A significant part of what we consider imperfect about our world was present before any moral responsibility and sin. An explanation for this, some would claim, is that long before humanity arrived, creation was spoiled by the devil, who is also one of God's creatures, albeit not from this world. In the view of many, including myself, this creates more problems than it solves, and we must look elsewhere.[1]

Incidentally, while it may not be possible to speak of the Fall as an historical event before which everything was perfect, it is still appropriate to regard the world as presently 'fallen', for there is a downward step between the glory of the source, who is God, and that of creation, which is not God.

We have no experience of creating *anything* from nothing, let alone a universe. 'Nothing' is a rather recalcitrant medium to work with. Strictly it is not a medium at all, of course. So we are in no position to know whether it is logically possible for God to create a perfect universe from nothing without a process which permits pain and suffering.

This by no means solves the problem of suffering. More will need to be said on that later. But it does offer a fruitful way to try to begin to understand creation. As has been described earlier, because the creation is not God, and because it is created for its own sake, for its own freedom and integrity, God is not obvious in the world. Given that, there is no particular reason why God's creation from nothing must immediately be perfect.

In this respect, the opening of the book of Genesis is especially intriguing:

> In the beginning when God created the heavens and the earth, the earth was a formless void and darkness covered the face of the deep, while a wind from God swept over the face of the waters. Then God said, 'Let there be light' . . . (Genesis 1.1–3a)

While the rest of the chapter is the story of everything being made good, here, at the first moment of creation, is chaos and disorder. Sweeping or hovering over this is a wind from God, or the spirit of God. And then God speaks his word, saying not 'Be light', but 'Let there be light.' All told there is a sense, not of total command and control, but of giving space and freedom, of bringing what is good from the deepest darkness by permitting word and gentle spirit. For it seems that it is not possible to create light without at the same time creating chaos and darkness from which it must be drawn.

It would be unwise to build too much on these debated verses alone. In what I will shortly go on to say about the Spirit, I will draw on the greater understanding that has come through Christ. We have already seen a hint of that in the rather comparable scene where the Spirit descends on Jesus in the water and God calls him 'my Son'. The more one tries to present the faith as a coherent whole, the more one realizes that to understand each part it is necessary to understand all the other parts, leaving the difficulty of where to start. I must therefore ask the reader to trust that the steps which I omit here will be filled in later. To tell the story of Jesus first would cause more difficulty, I think, through not having considered how God works in creation by his Spirit.

While the world could not be what it is now except by a process through time, we should not imagine that 'the creation' was just what happened at the beginning. The only reason anything exists now is because it is created *now*. The world is not a machine, or even an organism, that God set up and then left to follow its own laws. God is present to all things as their active source; not just all things bright and beautiful, but the bullet on its trajectory and the cancer as it grows. On the other hand, God is not creating the world like a moving image on a computer screen, where every pixel is coloured independently such that he may will any pattern and story with absolute control and no constraint. God does not design earthquakes, viruses or car accidents. The world has its own freedom.

We should think of the existence of the universe as precarious, like an unstable equilibrium. It is always on the edge. Some people want to see God as the deliberate will planning every individual event, but if the world were like that it would be absorbed into him. Others see no sign of God anywhere, but without him all would collapse back into disorder, chaos and then nothing. This should shake our sense of permanence about things. Only by God's faithfulness, new every morning, does life go on. We may not expect to find ourselves on the ceiling when we wake, but it should be a cause of wonder that order remains. After all, there is no science saying *why* anything should continue. Science only tells me *how* things have been, and will be if nothing changes.

The key to creation is where we began – with an understanding of the gratuitous existence of all things. Everything is a gift, and everything is to be given. Everything calls for a response, and everything is to be a response. Everything is word to the other, for everything is spoken into existence by God. God's presence as Spirit is not as the ground, source or origin of our being. The Spirit is not God present *to* us but God *between* us, as the one who can enable the word to be heard and as the one who can enable the response to be given, a draw towards God's life, but without compulsion. I am not saying that the Spirit is God *in* the world, in the sense of sharing our environment. The Spirit is not physically located or dispersed, for the Spirit is not physical. The Spirit is not another 'thing' in the world, but rather, the Spirit's presence means that the act of creation is not merely the calling into existence of individual elements but the energizing of responsiveness between one part of creation and every other. To risk some illustration, God is the author of the play *and* the director on the stage; the manufacturer of the engine *and* the fuel within; the one who molds the dust *and* the added breath.

And this is a presence at every level; not just between people, but between the smallest elements of matter; not just between individuals of similar level, but between each part at every level, and every other part at every level, including the whole. This is not to personalize all matter. The form of response may vary, and the degree of freedom may vary, but all matter is responsive. When I bang my head against the wall, it usually hits back – by the enabling of the Spirit.

The only reason anything exists in creation is because by the Spirit the Word was heard which called it into existence. From nothing came the chaos, and now everything is still being drawn from darkness into light. It is not that the Word formed the world and then the Spirit added a new, freer dimension of existence. Such thinking tends towards the misleading opposition of Word and Spirit as form and freedom – a danger raised by the illustrations of the play, engine and body listed earlier. Any form is enabled by the Spirit, for only through the Spirit is it possible for the Word to be heard. And any freedom is permitted by the Word, without whom the Spirit could not enable any response, for all freedom is a response to the Word. There is an analogy in physical matter itself, since Einstein has shown that energy is not an extra to the form, but an equivalence to the mass.

I have so far managed to avoid the need to use any personal pronouns for the Spirit. That is not to deny the Christian understanding of the Spirit as *God* the Spirit. It is rather to avoid any impression that the Spirit is known *to us* as personal. The Spirit's work is not to speak but to enable the Word to be heard. The Spirit between us does not speak for us but allows us our voice. This reticence of the Spirit is necessary for our freedom, so that the Word does not compel, and so that it is truly *our* response.

It is necessary to think further about the freedom of creation. There was a time in the history of science when the universe was thought to be governed by rigid deterministic laws which made the future closed. Human choice must be an illusion and God's action is limited to setting the laws in the first place.

This all changed with the development of quantum mechanics and chaos theory. According to quantum mechanics there is an essential unpredictability at the root of matter. At the scale of the smallest physical particles the world is very strange. Niels Bohr, one of the pioneers of quantum theory, once said that anyone who doesn't get dizzy when they think about it hasn't understood it. That remains true. It is a strangeness we don't normally meet directly, but it allows a tiny probability that one day when I bang my head against the wall it will respond by letting me through.

Chaos theory has to do with the unpredictability of certain complex systems at any level, the weather being the classic example. The level of precision with which conditions need to be known *now* in order to predict accurately beyond a certain time in the future is so high that you are forced down to the scale of quantum unpredictability.

Both these phenomena imply an openness in the sense that the future is unpredictable. And this is not simply due to a limitation in human knowledge or computing power. It is really the case that, even staying within the known laws of physics, the response which the different parts of the world make to each other is to some degree open and free.

This does not itself give an explanation of human freedom. We have already considered the fundamental difficulty science has with understanding our minds. But it does indicate that the problem with understanding how our minds can emerge from matter is not that matter allows no freedom. And if matter has this strangeness, inconceivable to earlier generations, what other truth may it bear, yet undiscovered or beyond the scope of physical scientific enquiry, which may allow us to be persons?

We should be careful not to speak of these phenomena as gaps which allow God's intervention in the world. God's action in creation is not that of intervention at all. Whether we think of God present to us or God present between us, God is not an agent sharing our environment, stepping in according to circumstances to seize an opportunity. The significance of these phenomena is the freedom of response they give to the world. They allow more freedom in the response for which God calls, but God's action is of the same kind whatever the circumstances. He is never more or less active.

How then may God act in providence? That is, to see where creation may go and to act to lead it forwards. Has this not been essential to the argument from the start: that God may work salvation? How may a prayer ever be answered? How may a miracle happen? How may God work providentially in apparently 'ordinary' events? Part of the answer is in what we have seen of the freedom of creation at lower levels – it is not a determined system where the future is fixed by the initial conditions. But an even greater degree of freedom is given in human responsibility.

From quantum mechanics and chaos theory, and from much other scientific knowledge, we know that the universe is an immensely complex system of interaction, where the whole affects each part and each part affects the whole, from the smallest scale to the largest. This is only what one may expect when gift and response is the premise. We know this equally from human relationships, where what we become, notwithstanding our freedom of will, is shaped by our history of relationship with others, as we are creative word to each other. For example, the more graciously we have been addressed during our lives, the more inclined we will have become to be gracious ourselves. We know also that humanity and the environment are shaped by each other.

God's overall purpose is that creation should be a faithful response to the Word, by each being a faithful response to the other. So, if the Spirit is always there seeking to enable our response by being between us and the other, the Spirit is always between us and the future. It is the Spirit who draws us on and gives us hope. The degree of freedom to respond which humans have is greater than that of any other part of creation we know. It is therefore through humanity that freedom can come to the world, and that by an openness to the enabling of the Spirit.

This means that it is necessary to be open for the Spirit within to change us. The Spirit is in me, not as an alternative centre of control, but as a presence *between* every part of me, the dynamic which holds me together as a body of interrelated parts. To be made whole is to come to a harmony of mutual response within. But this cannot happen without my neighbour, in relation with whom I may grow towards my own healing. And so on, to the whole world.

Because we are interrelated, the more true our response, the more it makes possible other truthful response. And we should not limit this to what we can explain, to the causal connections we can follow. If living and prayer is faithful, how can we say what difference it may not make? It cannot be a simple relationship between the fervency of the prayer or the faithfulness of life and its effectiveness since the world is complex. Some things may be impossible, no matter how much faith a person or a community has, without freedom being released by another part of creation. But it is not true either that prayer cannot work, or that prayer is about changing God's mind.

In thinking like this we should not separate humanity from the rest of the world. There are obvious direct ways in which we shape our world. But our faithfulness or otherwise may also affect the physical world in less direct ways, some of which we may notice and some of which we may not. It is for this reason that miracles are possible.

God's way with the world is to hold in being what the world's response has allowed. The Word is spoken and the Spirit is given, and what comes to be is what the world has made itself by its history of response. The integrity which God respects is the world's freedom, *not* scientific laws for themselves. It is not the respecting of order as in a machine, but the giving of space as in the harmony of music, or discord if we choose. (As we have observed, the trend in physics has been in this direction.) After all, this gratuitous creation is essentially a work of art, so we should expect surprises; it is always possible to draw out something new. If the Spirit is leading us forwards and things are not always going to be as they are now, we may expect occasional glimpses of the future to break in. And there is no reason why the 'laws' of the future should be the same as those of today.

It is therefore misleading to call miracles 'supernatural'. Miracles are natural in that they have been made possible by this world. When miracles happen, nothing is interrupted or overridden, and God has not intervened or exercised special power. They are remarkable, of course, as are many other things in life which show us how the world could be different. Miracles are not ordinary, by definition, but they are natural, in the same way that the future is natural. When we speak of 'the supernatural' or of 'intervention' we risk implying that God overrides creation's freedom, or that God could be more involved in the world than he normally is, or that he is always free to help people with miracles but rarely chooses to.

We do not have a God's-eye view of the world, but if we did, we would not see miracles as an interruption of his logic, but as a part of his logic, just as we now have such a perspective on solar eclipses compared with primitive cultures. Not that I am implying that scientific method could yield such a perspective on miracles. Here there is a higher logic than science can apprehend. A miracle is not so much a coincidence within a regular system, but a sign that the regularity we know has within it a straining towards a freer regularity.

Furthermore, the divine viewpoint would not reveal God to be more active providentially in miracles compared with other times. It is rather the case that God's active will is often more visible *to us* in the miraculous than at other times. From God's perspective there is not a 'natural' logic to the world which is occasionally suspended. There is what there is, always created through the Word and the Spirit, and always made possible by the world's response.

We have already considered how the arts are a particular focus and sign of the gratuitousness of life and the universe, and the logic of music is a good illustration of this. Bach's *Goldberg Variations*, for example, form a highly structured piece, tied down, one might think before hearing it, by an unchanging 'fundamental bass'. Yet there is invention and fresh imagination with each variation, and wonderful surprise. Each variation has its place and is made possible by what has gone before, but is not simply determined by it. This is the logic of creation. Interestingly, the *Variations* were written to be *useful* as a keyboard 'practice-piece', but there is such excess.

Part of what I have been describing may be expressed succinctly using the words of Austin Farrer: 'God not only makes the world, he makes it make itself.'[2]

This is another way of saying that God respects the world's freedom and integrity. Not that each element simply has fixed rules about how it may respond. When God 'makes' it is more mysterious, for a true response can open up new possibilities of response, and we cannot foresee what they may be.[3]

Furthermore, there is mystery in saying both that God makes the world *and* that the world makes itself. For this is not to divide the work by saying that God does part of the creating and the world does the rest. There is nothing that happens that is not God's doing, and nothing that is not the world's doing. The reason this is not contradictory is that God's action is not in the environment of the world's action and is therefore not in competition with it. This is God's way of pure service which was discussed earlier – his action is never as a force opposing any force in the world. God makes the world by his Word and Spirit such that there is freedom of response for the world itself. A faint analogy of this is found in the work of a novelist. At one level it seems that the writer is in complete control, and able to do what he or she likes, but at the same time the plot cannot be forced. Because the characters act according to who they are and according to their environment, the world of the book is also, in a sense, in control.

This may raise again the question of how we may know anything about God if he is not one of the players on the stage. And the answer is that if the world were not going anywhere new, if there were never any experience of salvation, if there were no sense that the whole environment was on the way to greater freedom, then we would be in the dark. If we look into the depths of a busy swimming pool, all we can see is the chaotic water, but when there is calm it becomes clear that there is a floor giving support. There are times when only the confusion of the world is visible, but faith has been made possible by those moments when God's purpose has become visible on the surface.

The fact that anything exists can point us to something ultimate that we may call 'God' – we look down seeing only water, and wonder how water alone can give support – but it is only an experience of salvation that can reveal a God who can be trusted. It is for this reason that Judaism stood out from other ancient religions by viewing time as linear, not cyclical, since it proclaimed a faith that God is a Saviour who can deliver the world from having to remain the way it has been.

The future of the whole world is therefore in our hands as well as in God's hands. The creation waits for humanity to allow God to bring it to know the freedom of living as useless gifts to each other, so that the whole may be set free for a new order. We now know how salvation *may* be possible, and we can already see the glory and freedom of God in much of creation and human life. But given so much that is still wrong, can we really hope to save ourselves? The Spirit sets us free from one vicious circle, whereby we could not receive the Word at all, whereby nothing could even exist. There is now a degree of light which enlightens everyone. But are we now found in another vicious circle, since we can only be free *together*? You need me to be free in order to be free yourself, and vice versa. For unless the rest of the world is free, the word I hear from that world – the word which shapes me into what I am – cannot be wholly faithful and true. And only the truth can set me free. How may this circle be broken?

6 Jesus of Nazareth

There are always a few people who deny that Jesus ever even existed. After all, there is very little corroborative evidence of the events of the Gospels available from independent sources. So a sceptic may say that the records are unreliable because they were written by Christians, who cannot be expected to have been objective.

This takes us back immediately to the question of trust. If we take a line that everything, or rather every*one*, is doubted until we have proof, then we are less than human. That is not to ask for a suspension of critical faculties. It is a basic human openness which requires a reason before doubting, not a reason before trusting. To dismiss the Gospels outright is therefore contrary to normal standards of historical research. Furthermore, it is a myth that history can ever be written without an agenda, and I say that without being derogatory.

Jesus was a Jew, born when Judaea was under Roman occupation, and beginning his ministry when Pontius Pilate was governor of the province. With their troubled history, present humiliation and internal strife, the Jewish people could not have been more aware of their need for deliverance. They lived expectantly, clinging to the hope given by their prophets of a Messiah who would overcome their enemies, reign in Jerusalem, and establish them to live peacefully in their own land.

Announced by John the Baptist, Jesus arrived on the scene proclaiming: 'The time is fulfilled, and the kingdom of God has come near; repent, and believe in the good news' (Mark 1.15). He travelled around, teaching about life under the freedom of God's rule, and through a ministry of compassion, often accompanied by miracles of healing, signs of that future freedom were made visible.

This would have been enough in itself for Jesus to appear significant, but a new dimension is revealed by the way he taught. There was a focus on himself, not so much by the content of his message, but by the authority he claimed. In the Sermon on the Mount he repeatedly stresses, 'You have heard that it was said . . . But I say to you' (e.g. Matthew 5.21f.). Of himself he claims: 'The Son of Man has authority to forgive sins' (Matthew 9.6); 'The Son of Man is lord even of the sabbath' (Mark 2.28); and 'The wedding-guests cannot fast while the bridegroom is with them, can they?' (Mark 2.19). When challenged about mixing with disreputable people, he replied, 'I have come to call not the righteous but sinners' (Mark 2.17). He called people to follow *himself* and to enter the kingdom at *his* invitation.

Now at this point a critic could argue that this is just the kind of gloss which the Church might add for its own purposes in order to build Jesus into something more than was evident from the real narrative of his life. The debate and scholarship around this issue is endless, and no justice can be done to it here, but the pressure against stripping away Jesus' miracles and authority as extraneous is this: if all that Jesus did was to tell people to love God and each other, why ever did his followers come to find such significance in his *person*, in who he himself was, and not just in his message?

One of the best summaries of Jesus' teaching concerning the life of the kingdom may be found in his most frequently recorded saying, and surely one of the least disputed. It occurs in all four Gospels, in slightly different forms: twice in Matthew and Luke; six in total, covering four different scenes: 'For those who want to save their life will lose it, and those who lose their life for my sake will find it.'[1]

Life is a gift to be given, and life itself is found in the giving of it. In view of what I said in the previous chapter about giving and response throughout all creation, it is worthwhile to note in passing that in John's Gospel Jesus illustrates this by reference to the natural world: 'unless a grain of wheat falls into the earth and dies, it remains just a single grain; but if it dies, it bears much fruit' (John 12.24).

If we look at the shape of the life of Jesus we find an extraordinary congruence with this heart of his teaching. He spoke of God in a way no one else did, as 'my Father' or 'Abba', a term of great intimacy, unthinkable for other Jews to use at the time, and going well beyond the occasional Old Testament description of God as father in relation to Israel. What this expressed was his complete dependence on God, and his understanding of his life as wholly given up to doing his Father's will, in fulfilment of his calling as the one through whom the kingdom would be inaugurated. For Jesus understood himself to be the Messiah, the Christ.

The movement of the Gospels is towards Jerusalem, the city of David, on which the expectations of Israel as a kingdom were focused. Two of the scenes (and four of the references) where the above saying is made are in the context of Jesus speaking of his coming death. At Caesarea Philippi, he asks his disciples, 'Who do people say that the Son of Man is?' 'You are the Christ,' Simon Peter replies. Jesus goes on to speak of how he must suffer, and be killed, and be raised. What Jesus expects is exactly in accordance with what he has believed, taught and lived. But for the disciples there is confusion: the Messiah was meant to be someone who arrived in Jerusalem and triumphed.

Significantly, it was just before Passover when Jesus rode into Jerusalem, when people were gathering for the feast to celebrate God's deliverance of Israel from slavery in Egypt. The crowds went before him shouting, 'Hosanna to the Son of David.' It was both a cry of praise and a call for salvation. However, the place to which Jesus brought his challenge was not the Roman praetorium but the Jewish temple, and with direct action, parable and teaching, he passed devastating, fearless judgement on the religious leaders for the way they used other people's lives to save their own. In view of his popularity, they could only see this as a threat to their position. If necessary, his life must be lost in order to protect their own. So by the time of the Passover meal, plans were in place for the arrest of Jesus.

> . . . Jesus . . . took a loaf of bread, and when he had given thanks, he broke it and said, 'This is my body that is for you. Do this in remembrance of me.' In the same way he took the cup also, after supper, saying, 'This cup is the new covenant in my blood. Do this, as often as you drink it, in remembrance of me.' (1 Corinthians 11.23–25)

The first covenant had been established when Moses read the law in the hearing of all the people, and sprinkled them with the blood of a sacrificed animal. The temple rested on these principles of law and sacrifice. Now Jesus points to himself as the sacrifice, recalling the prophecy of Jeremiah concerning a new covenant when God's law will be written on the heart, just as Ezekiel had spoken of the new age when the Spirit within would change hearts of stone to hearts of flesh.

That night, after Jesus had been arrested and brought to trial before the high priest and the council, the witnesses against him, whom the chief priests had eventually drawn from out of the people, claimed that he had spoken against the temple. It was a shrewd move to deflect criticism from themselves by portraying Jesus as a threat to the symbol of their national identity. Early in the morning Jesus was handed over to Pilate, who delivered him to be crucified.

The body of Jesus was wrapped in linen and placed in a tomb that had been cut out of rock, belonging to Joseph of Arimathea, a member of the council. A stone was rolled against the entrance of the tomb.

Early on the first day of the week, while it was still dark, Mary Magdalene came to the tomb and saw that the stone had been removed and the body was missing. Later, as she stood weeping, Jesus appeared and called her by name, after which she went and announced to the disciples, 'I have seen the Lord.' This is just one of the numerous Gospel records of appearances of Jesus over many days to different groups of disciples. The apostle Paul also assembles a list of witnesses to the appearance of Jesus, to explain to the church at Corinth that this is the testimony by which they had come to believe.

That is the New Testament history of Jesus of Nazareth, in the barest outline, and it is no substitute for reading the Gospels themselves. The subsequent history of the first disciples and the Church poses a question. If it is *not* true that Jesus was raised from the dead, what did happen?

We should bear in mind that the above records were written very much within living memory. It is true that the accounts of the appearances of Jesus cannot be altogether harmonized, but that tends to make the essence of them more credible since there has clearly been no attempt to force everything to be consistent. Further evidence of authenticity is the reliance on women as witnesses, hardly convincing in that culture. And there is clear harmony on the fundamental claims that Jesus was buried, that the tomb was found empty, and that he was seen alive by the disciples.

We can be sure that the same disciples who had been with Jesus were the first to hold the belief that he had been raised from the dead. But if Jesus was not raised, what had convinced them otherwise? It is hard to imagine that they could become collectively deluded, as some have suggested. And it is impossible to imagine what motive anyone could have to be deceitful, especially when we think of the price these disciples would come to pay for their faith.

We should not underestimate how unlikely a source of good news the story of Jesus was at the point of his burial. To proclaim a *crucified* Messiah was not a promising way to gather a following. To a Jew, this was not so much a sign of anointing but of cursing; the most degrading and humiliating death imaginable. It is hard to believe that the disciples would have been inclined to continue to see Jesus as a saviour without the most convincing evidence that he really had been raised bodily from the dead.

It is therefore important to see that it is very difficult to come up with an alternative explanation. There certainly does not exist any theory which looks at all convincing, despite the best efforts to find one.

But I say that without the expectation that every reasonable reader should necessarily become convinced. I can imagine a circumstance where a number of reliable people bear witness to something quite extraordinary, where there is no apparent alternative explanation, and yet I would not find it sufficient evidence to commit myself. A UFO sighting, for example, where they were all sure they actually *saw* the little green aliens at the windows. I think I would reserve judgement.

The point is that the credibility of the Christian faith is not built on first establishing a watertight historical proof of the resurrection. It matters that a persuasive case can be made, and that it is not merely a theoretical possibility. But the fact of the resurrection cannot be separated from its significance. If Jesus was raised, what does that mean? In this book I am trying to show how everything connects; that through Jesus so many of the pieces may be seen to fall into place; that it is, if you like, the best interpretation of life and the universe, not just of the Gospel resurrection narratives. The first Christians came to believe that Jesus really is the Saviour of the world. For such a claim to be plausible it matters that somewhere, somehow, it can be seen that the world is being saved. It is of the essence of the good news that its witnesses may not claim power as disclosers of a public truth or a reasoned proof, but must rather live out this salvation by taking the place of servants.

7 Recognizing Jesus

We can appreciate how the appearances of Jesus would have confirmed the belief of the disciples that Jesus was the Christ. They would then assume, we may quickly think, that the point of his death and resurrection was to demonstrate who he was by a miraculous sign, before continuing with his mission of deliverance. They could have continued to hold this view after the ascension, when they no longer saw him, for they believed he would soon return to restore the kingdom. A Messiah who had proved his invulnerability to death would strike fear into the heart of any ruler whose power depended on being able to dispose of people.

Instead, they began to recognize that the death and resurrection of Jesus were not a prelude to the real mission, but the real mission itself. Jesus had spent his ministry teaching them that the path to life was the giving of your own life. When they had asked him if they could share in his glory, he had simply told them that they must share in his suffering. He had taught them, and shown them, that he had come to serve, not to be served. He knew God intimately as Father, and taught them to pray the same way; but that meant giving your life up to the Father's will.

At the same time, he had spoken as if his own words had the same authority as the Law. He had said that *he* had authority to forgive sins, bypassing the temple. He had shown at the Passover meal that *his* death was to be the sacrifice through which the new covenant would be made. He would not be the kind of Messiah they expected, who would establish and uphold peace so that the temple and the Law alone could be the rule by which people lived, instead of the Roman jurisdiction. He would himself embody the Law which God had spoken; the temple, where God was present; and the sacrifice which made them God's people.

How could the paradox be resolved? On the one hand, Jesus was the perfect servant, and completely dependent on God. On the other hand, the significance of everything he did was because of who he was; he was effectively *as God* to people.

Debate on the understanding of this continued through several centuries, but the New Testament shows that from very early times Jesus is given the highest honour. For example, in one of Paul's letters written about twenty years after the death of Jesus, we read this: 'there is one God, the Father, from whom are all things and for whom we exist, and one Lord, Jesus Christ, through whom are all things and through whom we exist' (1 Corinthians 8.6). Here, as on several other occasions, Jesus is portrayed as the creator.

We do not know exactly how this recognition of the person of Jesus developed, but we can be sure that it did so within the Jewish thinking of the first Christians, who were firmly centred in the belief in one God. This is important, for it means that there would have been great resistance to thinking of Jesus as divine, unless they had encountered something much more significant than great teaching and impressive miracles. Monotheism, we should note, was not a statement about the nature of God himself, but a claim that he has no rivals. And it was not necessary to look further than their own Scriptures to develop their understanding of God.

We have already seen from the Old Testament that God is someone who speaks his word, making himself known in creation and in the giving of the law. It was therefore natural to speak of Jesus as word, but now making a distinction in God. So John writes: 'In the beginning was the Word, and the Word was with God, and the Word was God ... All things came into being through him ... And the Word became flesh and lived among us, and we have seen his glory ...' (John 1.1, 3, 14). It is worth noting that the word translated 'lived' alludes precisely to God's glory dwelling in the temple.

We have heard from the Psalms of the Lord's decree concerning the anointed one who would take the throne of David: 'You are my son' (Psalm 2.7). On several occasions the New Testament writers quote or refer to this in relation to Jesus. The epistle to the Hebrews uses the title to show that Jesus is above the angels; not merely a messenger, but the one who makes visible God's very being. In conjunction with Jesus' own knowledge of God as Father, we can see how Jesus came to be spoken of as God's Son.

Of particular importance to the early Church, and quoted widely in the New Testament, was the second part of the prophecy of Isaiah, which speaks repeatedly of a servant who would be *as Israel*, yet, in contrast to the history of the people, would never be rebellious.[1]

They were not easy passages to apply to a Messiah, because while this servant will be 'exalted and lifted up, and shall be very high' (Isaiah 52.13), he will also suffer. Yet the early Christians would not fail to notice that just the same language of being exalted and lifted up is used in Isaiah's vision of God. So John, for example, strikingly says that what Isaiah saw was the glory of *Jesus*.[2]

Gradually the words were found to describe what it meant to have known Jesus as both a suffering, crucified servant and as the very action and word of God himself. God is not only a source of creation; he is the source of the Word, who is himself God, who reveals and reflects the source. God is not only a father to Israel; he is the Father who begets the Son, who is himself God, who responds by glorifying the Father.

Earlier, in Chapter 4, we considered what it might mean if God revealed himself as a saviour, and was therefore trusted. It made it possible to come to understand God as one who, all apart from creation, gave of himself and responded to himself. What that thinking anticipates, and what the Old Testament was reaching towards, is revealed in Jesus Christ.

But here is something completely new, which we did not reckon with earlier. The revelation that God in himself is gift and response was not revealed through Jesus merely by him teaching it as a spiritual truth, as a prophetic insight. It was revealed because he was himself God, the Word made flesh. How may that be reconciled with all I have said before about God being 'other'; about God not sharing our environment? How may it be reconciled with understanding Jesus also to be human?

The early Church debated this over centuries, guided by two clear principles: for Jesus to be the *saviour*, he must be fully God; for Jesus to be *our* saviour, he must be fully human. (Note that, as always, what drives this is the experience of God as one who saves.) *How* Jesus can save us is another question we have not yet considered, and when we do, it will become clear why these principles matter. But first we must consider Jesus as a person who is fully God and fully human.

8 Jesus – God and Man

If it were only necessary to say that Jesus is fully human, then no further explanation would be required. We are familiar with humanity. But once we say that he is fully God, we want to ask: what is it about Jesus that makes him divine? We shall eventually see that the 'what' form of this question sets us on the wrong track. However, it is instructive to stay with it and discover all the blind alleys; the places where we will *not* find the divinity of Jesus.

The Gospels of both Matthew and Luke tell us that Mary was a virgin when the child was conceived. We may immediately think that this is the gap which allows space for God. Perhaps the origin of Jesus was half human and half divine? Put like that, we quickly see why it won't do. Jesus was not a hybrid, but *fully* human and *fully* God. The New Testament writers, and most theologians today, make no significance of the virginal conception as something essential to the divinity of Jesus, though it was a sign, as we have seen other miracles to be, that the future has something new to bring.

Again, as with other miracles, it is not necessary to regard the birth of Jesus as supernatural. It was God's action, as everything is God's action (none of us was conceived but by the Holy Spirit), but it was made possible by the history of this world. This was creation's order, not an intervention to disturb it. In the words of Rowan Williams, it was 'nature itself opening up to its own depths'.[1]

The faith of Israel developed in response to God by the enabling of the Spirit. This faith came, not because they were given more opportunity by special divine provision – God is present in essentially the same way to all peoples – but because it happened to be along this historical line that a trust grew such that the future could be made more

open. God does not show partiality. He works to draw all people towards greater faith, but he does this in the circumstances of people's
lives, not through a direct bypass, and these circumstances vary from
one to another, making faith more or less likely. God always works
providentially, but along this thread, because of where it led, it is more
evident to us.

And so we come to the point where Mary says to the angel, 'Here am
I, the servant of the Lord, let it be with me according to your word.'
There is no overriding of creation. Rather, the history of the world, and
in particular the history of Israel, has led to this moment. Now, only by
the remarkable faith of Mary, and enabled by the Spirit, the creation is
opened to new light.[2]

It is of course true that this *incarnation*, the becoming flesh of the
Word, was a wonderful miracle: an extraordinary, unique event which
was the action *of God*. But it was also *of this world*, in the sense that from
the very beginning it was always the world's potential future, always
something which the world could say 'Yes' to, and *itself* make possible.
And as we shall see, it was always something which the world *needed* to
say 'Yes' to, and still needs to if creation is to be brought to fulfilment. If
God is himself free gift and response, and creation is to reflect that glory,
how can this, the greatest gift to the world, ever be thought of as something *imposed*? This was something which was always possible, but not
something which God could have done at any time. It happened 'when
the fullness of time had come' (Galatians 4.4).

If we cannot find the divinity of Jesus in the circumstances of his
birth, can we find it in his life, in the evidence of something *extra* to his
humanity? For example, when he raised the dead or opened the eyes of
the blind, did he not then act as God rather than as a man?

We cannot make this opposition, for there is nothing that Jesus did
that he did not do as a human being. He was a dependent creature, called
into being by God, praying to God, and enabled by the Holy Spirit in all
that was done by him and through him. Peter says just this concerning
the anointing of Jesus by the Holy Spirit, that he went about doing good
and healing because 'God was *with* him' (Acts 10.38).

The New Testament speaks of the presence of the Holy Spirit at all
stages in the life of Jesus. It is by the Spirit that he is conceived; the Spirit
descends on him at his baptism at the beginning of his public ministry;
by the Spirit he goes about doing good and healing; by the Spirit he
offers himself on the cross; and by the Spirit he is raised.[3]

But we should not imagine that his divinity consists in this unique degree to which the Spirit can work. The Spirit is there in the life of Jesus as God *between*, as in all creation, and this in itself is no different from God's way with other humans. What makes the *visible* difference here is the faith of Jesus, his complete trust in his Father. Jesus is therefore more fully human than any other man or woman, but still this does not make him God. We are all called to share in the same fullness such that we partake of the divine life, but we will never actually be God.

Jesus was a part of this creation, not in any way able to control or impose beyond what was humanly possible. So we read of an occasion when 'he could do no deed of power' (Mark 6.5) because of the unbelief of the people. Given what was said in Chapter 5, we can understand how it was possible for many miracles to occur in the ministry of Jesus, because of his openness to God and the future which he signalled, but we can also understand that there was much that was *not* possible.

Jesus was not superhuman in any way. He grew in knowledge as any other child; there were things he did not know; he grew weary. We should not imagine that he could not be sick, or that he was necessarily the best carpenter that the world has known. He was not above the world. Jesus was a first-century Jew from Nazareth, inheriting characteristics from Mary, shaped by his parents and friends, sharing Galilean culture.

Another temptation in trying to understand how Jesus can be fully God is to look inside him and to imagine that when we get to the centre, unlike us, it is really God who is in control, replacing the humanity. The history of the Church's thinking in the early centuries is one of progressive opposition to this approach. First there were those who said that Jesus only appeared to be human. Then some argued that the human soul of Jesus was replaced by God. And then, finally, there was debate over whether Jesus had a human will. But if Jesus is fully human, then he is human to the core, and the incarnation can in no way be thought of as overriding or replacing any part of the humanity.

John makes this clear in his Gospel: 'And the Word became flesh.' The Word was not alongside the flesh, or indwelling the flesh, or controlling the flesh. Flesh is what the Word became, but not by turning into flesh. Who is this flesh? The Word; fully God. What has the Word become? Flesh; fully man.

This helps us to see that the divinity and the humanity are not symmetrical, however much the terms may suggest that. 'God' does not denote a genus of being like 'human'. If we ask *who* Jesus is, we should answer 'the Word' or 'God the Son'. If we ask *what* Jesus is, we should answer 'human'.

Has this helped? Only if asking *who* a person is has any meaning apart from describing *what* they are. Part of the difficulty with understanding the incarnation is that we don't really understand our own selves. What is it that determines our personal identity? What is it that makes me *who* I am, the *same* person who was born all those years ago?

A traditional answer would be the soul, thought of as a detachable, immaterial, immortal part of us. There is no biblical or scientific reason to believe this, though use of the word 'soul' is still helpful in other ways. We are made of matter, of dust, and it is by the work of the Spirit of God that we have life, not because there is any part of our being which transcends this creation.

We may then think that it is the body which holds our identity, but this has two problems. First, you cannot seriously claim to have used the same brush for twenty years if it has had three new handles and two new heads. Our bodies are in no less a state of flux. As C. S. Lewis vividly put it, 'My form remains one, though the matter in it changes continually. I am, in that respect, like a curve in a waterfall.'[4]

Second, if we believe in life beyond the grave, what will make me the same person, when the new body will be made of completely different stuff?

Another suggestion has been the *form* of our being, an 'information-bearing pattern'[5] that is holistic, including our memories and personality, which can be held by God even after death. This solves some problems, but seems to reduce us to an impersonal set of qualities, giving up on the personal as significant at all. Is my identity essentially a very long binary digit? Is to be *like* me to be the *same person* as me? Essential to being a person is that I am not an instance of something. I am not repeatable.

Many who approach this question without a faith perspective say that the search for something that gives continuity of personal identity for humans is just as hopeless as for brushes. We are our bodies. We will not find anything *about* ourselves that answers this question. When we speak of ourselves as persons, as if there is a self, an 'I' which is substantial and continuous, then it is an illusion, even if we accept that we have free will. We are living matter which has the quality of consciousness, but there is no 'real me' who is independent of this particular body, who could exist as a different body.

There is an important truth here which we have a good reason not to resist. Later we will think about God as Trinity, and see that the persons of the Father, the Son and the Holy Spirit have their being only in the relationships in which each is held. God is not a society of persons who *have* relationships. In our society, we tend to think of ourselves first as persons who then also have relationships. But in God, the relationships are prior. The Father is not a divine being who happens to have a Son. The Son is eternally begotten of the Father, which means that this action (which is God's life, and not a past event) constitutes who God is; it is in the eternal begetting of the Son that the Father has his being. And what is true of the Father is true, each in a different way, of the Son and the Spirit.

In a similar, though not identical, way we cannot find anything that makes us substantial as persons without considering our relation to God. I will never find inside myself, or in the form of myself, anything that names me, that makes me a person and not merely a conscious, responsive body. By myself, I cannot know that 'I' exist. The notion of an immortal soul is both an escape from dependence on our bodies and an escape from dependence on God. On the other hand, to give up on the personal, or to reduce it to a 'pattern', is to diminish ourselves, and certainly to make the incarnation impossible.

Unlike God, we are objects as well as subjects. As objects, we are bodies. Some think that we are only objects – bodies which have the qualities of being conscious and responsive. But if we are also continuous, real subjects, or *persons*, then there is a truth about us which cannot be objectified or reduced to a quality. I am a some*one* and not just a some*thing*; a *who* as well as a *what*. We would be right to think of this as an illusion if we did not trust that God calls us by name. Only in relation to God do I become *who* I am. We are made personal by God through his relating to us personally.

Similarly, only in relation to God was Jesus who he was, not because of something special about his humanity. From the moment of conception, by the call of God, the Word is *who* this flesh was, and therefore flesh is what the Word had become. Throughout the life of Jesus, all of the presence, experience, action and speech of this flesh were the presence, experience, action and speech of the Word, yet all were human. The person of Jesus was God the Son living as a man. It can therefore be seen that the full divinity of Jesus in no way makes his humanity different from ours. The answer to *who* we are, rather than *what* we are, is different for every one of us, and it is here where the divinity of Jesus is found.

Or rather, it is here where we see that the divinity of Jesus cannot be 'found' at all. If you are thinking that there is something important unexplained in all this, then you are right. It would be foolish to claim to have explained the incarnation. When I speak of God's 'relation' to us by which we become who we are, I accept that it seems conveniently inscrutable. However, the fact that the personal is something which cannot be located or analyzed is itself the point. By definition, the minute we think we have found it, we should find that we have lost it. You cannot objectify what is *not* objective. It is the image of God in us, and therefore, like God, can only be received in each other as a gift and never grasped as a product of our own thinking. The Son, whom Paul speaks of as 'the image of the invisible God' (Colossians 1.15), revealed the truth about human beings, who are made in the image of God, as well as the truth about God.

There may still be a niggling doubt about whether Jesus really was human like us, since it is held that Jesus was without sin, and that it matters that he was without sin. The New Testament makes this explicit and Jesus is portrayed as the Son who knows himself only as the Son, who lives only to do the Father's will. He is the Word and he is unfailingly true to who he is. Was Jesus therefore somehow removed from the desires and temptations that can afflict us? And how may this be reconciled with the conclusion at the end of Chapter 5 that we can only be free together; that we are trapped in a vicious circle? Is Jesus also removed from the influence of the corrupted word which we hear from the world?

One tradition in the Church has held that Jesus did not share our 'fallen humanity' but had an 'unfallen humanity' such as Adam possessed before his disobedience. It is difficult to make sense of this, not least within the overall understanding I am proposing here, where there is no such thing as 'unfallen humanity' because creation, including humanity, has not lost an initially perfect state. Jesus shared our nature, and we should not imagine that he was unaware of anything from within or without which was a draw to action which would not have been true. Do we not see such a tension in the garden of Gethsemane? However, we can discern within ourselves that, faced with the threat to our security which may accompany what is right, we may be aware of the possibility of unfaithful response, yet know that it is a step further to feed and give space to that wrong in our imaginations.[6]

Jesus fully shared our humanity, yet as the Son he remained true to the Father at all times. Being therefore completely free, he was able to remain free. Not being free, we are unable to overcome what is against us from within and without by ourselves. That Jesus was free from the beginning, and that we have never known ourselves to be free, is a difference. But it is a difference which remains within humanity.

Two final questions may come to mind. First, given all that has been stressed about God being 'other', not sharing our environment, is it not contradictory that he should become flesh? Second, isn't there a conflict between God the Son existing *both* in heaven *and* in the world?

These questions may be answered together. For when we say that God is other, we are saying that he does not have any environment. He is not *located* in heaven. He is completely free and unconstrained. When we imagine that God's eternal being and incarnate life are mutually exclusive, we only do so because we think in terms of 'two places at once'. But God himself is not *in* anything: temporal, physical or anything else. He is not even *in* 'a mode of existence', as some writers put it when addressing this issue. To say that God 'came down from heaven' is helpful imagery, but we should not imagine a literal change of environment. It is precisely because God is *other* that he is free to become incarnate. Paradoxically, the more God is considered to have a being of our kind, the less significant and the less possible the incarnation becomes.

9 Freedom through Jesus

What difference then does Jesus make to the world? This is the question we may now consider; but first a summary of the story so far.

God's life is self-giving and receiving for its own sake. This is more familiarly and elegantly expressed as 'God is love'. However, love is open to misinterpretation. We may miss its gratuitous nature. We can mistake mutual possession as love. God's love is about giving of one's *free* self for the sake of the other, without that other ever becoming the end of one's existence. To be free means not to have to justify one's existence.

From this freedom, and because of this freedom, God created the world. The world is not God, but because it is created by God, it must be 'of God', in the sense that it must reflect who he is. It must therefore be created *for* freedom, yet by its nature that freedom cannot ever be something imposed by intervention or control. The goal of creation is therefore to mirror the life of God, and to be 'of God' as the Son is begotten of the Father. But the Son is eternally begotten and free, whereas creation has a beginning from nothing, and cannot be instantly free. If creation is to be free, it must find its own freedom; it cannot be externally constructed without overriding freedom in the process.

The history and future of the world are therefore the history and future of its creation and salvation, which are one and the same. God 'lets' creation be through his Word, and the Spirit is a reticent presence *between*, drawing creation forward, enabling the Word to be heard, but not to compel; enabling the world to respond, but in its own voice; and in the same way enabling the world to hear and respond to itself.

The world which God now holds is therefore what it has become through its history of response. It is a world where we see both glorious freedom and horrific evil. What the world can become is limited only by its own response. In the web of relationships which comprise the universe, everything speaks and responds to the other, and each affects and is affected by the whole. Nowhere is the degree of freedom higher in the world than in human beings, who are therefore able either to allow God to bring creation to freedom or to prevent God from stopping its descent back into chaos.

How well is humanity doing? There are obvious evils to which we may point: war, starvation, preventable disease, oppressive regimes, exploitation of resources. We may narrow the focus to crime, breakdown in relationships, or specific moments in our own lives when we recognize, even on a daily basis, where we may slip through carelessness or worse.

But underlying all that is the deeper problem that we cannot really believe that we are created to be gifts: gifts in the sense that we don't have to justify our existence, and gifts in the sense that we are to give ourselves. Instead, we labour under a need to make ourselves significant, useful or approved. With that comes a complementary need to protect ourselves and the temptation to use others for our preservation. Subtly, or not, we therefore live in competition with each other. We fear others, especially those who are different. We restrict our openness, lest we make vulnerable the possessions or prejudices that keep us safe. We cannot believe that fullness of life is not found in seeking first the fullness of our own lives.

This sin pervades all life, including that part of it regarded as 'respectable'. It is the grain of the world, so much of the time we don't notice it, especially in ourselves. It is an inclination of our nature, and a product of our nurture. It is the word we receive from the world, and the word we give to the world. It is 'in each the work of all and in all the work of each'.[1]

We may therefore question whether humanity has the means to escape into freedom. We have freedom of will, but this is not to be understood as an absolute autonomy that allows us at any time to evaluate and choose from a range of options restricted only by our physical limits. What is possible for us depends on the person we have become and is therefore limited by what we have received from others. We cannot control at any moment what may occur to us or what we may desire. As I said earlier, in order to be free, we need to hear and receive the creative word which can shape us and set us free. But if none of us is free, and we are constantly shaped by each other, how can that word be heard? Where may a truthful response come from? Who may hear and faithfully respond, thereby opening creation such that, by the Spirit, yet more truthful response is made possible?

It is against this background that we begin to see the significance of Jesus, and the importance of acknowledging his full humanity and full divinity. For if Jesus were not a fully human part of this creation, how could he be the means by which we may be set free, since creation may only be set free by itself? And if he were not fully divine, how may he himself be free? So we shall see why, for creation and salvation to be made possible, it was necessary not just for God to be present *to us* and *between us*, but also for God to be present *as us*.

Jesus proclaimed a gospel of freedom, and was himself completely free. Not in the sense that he was independent and free of constraint. On the contrary, not only did he necessarily live within the limits of human existence, but he also gave himself constantly to his Father's will in response to the world which he served. His freedom was to know himself only as the Son, never seeking approval, never claiming advantage, never holding back anything of himself for the sake of his own security. Hence we see a combination of utter humility and assured authority, as, for example, in his willingness to mix with the outcasts of society without regard for the censure of the religious leaders.

These years of selfless service must in themselves be significant in opening creation, that the Spirit may enable it to move forwards. That is what we see in the miracles, and in the response by those who follow Jesus and hear his teaching. But the New Testament makes clear that the greater self-giving is yet to come.

Not surprisingly, those most receptive to Jesus were people who had no approval, advantage or security, like Mary Magdalene. But for others, as we have seen, Jesus could only be perceived as a threat. The presence of the incarnate Word himself was not sufficient for the light of the gospel to penetrate their walls of self-protection. On the contrary, this presence drew out their instinct for preservation of self by control of others. The attitudes of Jesus and his accusers are diametrically opposed. The world's lack of freedom is brought to an intense focus as it seeks to destroy its freest part; its only truly free part. The world demonstrates its capacity to annihilate itself by descent into chaos.

In this we see the *passion* of Jesus. He claims no ground and asserts no justification for himself. He remains free and given. In giving himself to the end, the life of God is supremely displayed on the cross. That is why the New Testament speaks of the cross as a place of *glory*.

Here the glory of God reaches to the heart of the chaos of the world. Jesus cries, 'My God, my God, why have you forsaken me?' (Mark 15.34). This does not suggest that God has actively abandoned Jesus. What would that say about God? It is rather an experience of God's absence, inevitable when in the grip of forces which God cannot intervene to do anything about, for God must remain true to his own freedom. God remains true to who he is, in both the Father's giving of himself to the world in the Son by the Spirit, and in the Son's giving of himself to the Father for the world by the Spirit.

Through a long history, God had been patiently lying in wait by his Spirit, gently breathing faith into life, faith that would breed more faith and open new possibilities. Through the trust of Israel, and its focus in Mary, the time had come for God to send his Son. Now the life of Jesus comes to its climax. Having never wavered in his complete trust in God, he offers himself wholly and perfectly unto death. What on earth may such a uniquely faithful response make possible?

This is how the difference is made. Here, through Jesus, creation opens itself to the new, and the future is able to break in as never before. The *end* is able to break in, as Christ is raised. Not restored *back* to life, but as the 'first fruits' (1 Corinthians 15.20) of the life of the age to come. Not merely raised psychologically in the minds of the disciples to be their inspiration, but raised bodily as the hope for the future of the matter of our world.

Furthermore, since there had been such a uniquely profound opening in the world (a world where all things are related at deeper levels than we can understand, such that a true response releases the possibility of further true response), the presence of the Spirit became evident in a fresh and abundant way. At the feast of Pentecost when the disciples are 'filled with the Holy Spirit' (Acts 2.4), Peter addresses the crowd and says that this is what was spoken through the prophet Joel: 'I will pour out my Spirit upon all flesh' (Acts 2.17). More anticipations of the end.

But has not the Spirit been present with all flesh from the beginning? Indeed, and everything that exists does so by the Spirit, but it is when the new comes that we notice the Spirit, as one who is always there to lead forward. And so, as creation is opened, from the world's perspective it is as if the Spirit is poured out.

The same Spirit in creation is now able to do something new. It is not without significance that the feast of Pentecost is the time for celebration of the giving of the law. The Spirit is present who would change hearts of stone for hearts of flesh, hearts on which the law would be written. The early Christians believed that they had been brought into this new kind of life which enabled them to know God as Jesus did. By the Spirit they could pray to God in the same way, saying 'Abba, Father' (Romans 8.15; Galatians 4.6). By the Spirit, Jesus was present with them. The disciples had received the promised 'power from on high' (Luke 24.49), a power which at its heart is the gift to live selflessly as Jesus did, a power not to need to grasp power.

Ten days before Pentecost, Jesus ascended into heaven, according to Luke, after showing himself alive over a period of 40 days. We cannot think literally of travel beyond the clouds into heaven, but this should not detract from the significance of the event. Here Jesus is exalted and made Lord, for through him creation can now be set free. Since no power of evil was able to overcome him, ultimately nothing can hold us in its grip. Not that we should imagine this to be the point where Jesus is at last able to wield power as we commonly know it. His rule is the paradoxical 'easy yoke' – the subjugation of subjugation itself.

Furthermore, the ascension tells us that the humanity of Jesus is not in the past, and therefore it tells us that our humanity has a future freedom. The risen Christ in his new humanity remains for ever a part of creation, as its future. Therefore, as the Spirit is between all parts of creation, so he is able to make Christ present to us, and make us united with him.

Or, to put it another way, by the Spirit the Word may be heard by us and create us to be like Christ. This is where we come full circle to the earlier point where I had to draw on the greater understanding that has come through Christ in speaking of the Spirit's work in creation. It is through Christ that we understand the Spirit to be the one who enables both the Word to be heard, and our 'Abba' response to be given. So all this work of *salvation* is coterminous with *creation*. Even Easter and Pentecost are not about God acting differently by more direct involvement or intervention. Rather, in all the events of the life of Christ, and especially in his cross, creation acts differently, and through God working as he always does, creation goes somewhere new. The reason why Christ brings to creation the hope of enjoying the freedom of God is grounded in an understanding of what kind of creation was necessary for freedom to be possible.[2]

It is a world which has real responsibility for itself. That is why the call to stand where Jesus stood, saying, 'Abba, Father', is not a call to the protection of infancy, but to the maturity of reflecting the Father's self-giving by being vulnerable in the world as Jesus was. The only place in the Gospels where Jesus is recorded praying 'Abba' is where he faces the cross in the Garden of Gethsemane.

So what difference does Jesus make? Through him the vicious circle is broken; the circle in which we were trapped, whereby we make each other *not* be free. The way is open for creation to go on to make itself new. As Christ gave himself, so by his Spirit he can enable us to give ourselves and know each other as free.

Clearly everything has not been immediately put right. To use the language of Paul, we still need to work out our salvation that God may work in us. What that means in practice, and for the future of the world, we will come to later.

10 Models of Atonement

Christians agree that Jesus is the way by which things may be put right. They do not always agree on how he has made this possible. While the Church in the early centuries debated the question of the person of Jesus, and clarified its belief with some precision, the same is not true concerning what Jesus has done. The debate has happened, but it has never been held necessary to lay down a definition. A number of explanations or 'models of atonement' have been developed over the years, some very influential and widespread. The New Testament, rather than give a theory or an explanation, tends to use a range of images drawn from the writers' own culture and history.

It may be argued that the *how* doesn't matter. Jesus did what was necessary, and that's all we need to know. There is some truth in that. Yet it surely ought to be possible to say something to an enquirer who asks 'How?' Also, it is not possible to pretend that different views on this never imply different, even contradictory, kinds of faith and practice. It is therefore helpful to make some comparison between the account I have given in the previous chapter, which I will refer to as the 'creation model', and the wider tradition.

Some have focused on the decisiveness of the incarnation, whereby we become associated with the divine life, assured of God's commitment to the world and enlightened to see all creation as sharing God's goodness. The cross is a compelling display of God's love, and the resurrection shows that this love is indomitable.

It is hardly possible to disagree with this, as far as it goes. And it does not conflict with the creation model unless it is claimed that no more needs to be said. But is it enough? Does it recognize the power of evil in the world as something which must be overcome? Does this not come close to the implausible claim that a powerful example of goodness is sufficient?

Another model sees the conflict with all the forces of evil as the heart of the matter. Christ is the victor who by his cross and resurrection has defeated everything which holds humanity in chains. Jesus entered the domain of darkness and death and exhausted the power of evil. By rising again, he broke open the gates of hell and released the captives.

Again, this is not incompatible with the creation model, for there we saw that the world needed to be set free from the vicious circle of its own mutual imprisonment. However, Christ's victory is sometimes also understood to be a triumph over the devil and spiritual forces of evil which come from beyond the world. Such language can help us to recognize the seriousness of evil as something that can hold us, even possess us. The danger comes when it is seen to remove the real struggle to somewhere away from the arena of human relationships.

Furthermore, this model does not itself give an explanation, more an image for what has happened. In some versions it is developed into a theory; the rather odd idea of tricking the devil, or the more biblical picture of redemption or payment of a ransom. In the creation model, it can certainly be said that Christ 'paid the price of sin' in order to set us free. But ransom cannot go beyond metaphor into explanation without having to consider the unacceptable notion of payment being made to the devil.

There is a third and most significant approach, in terms of its influence on the Church in the West at least. It is expressed in a range of forms, but at its heart is the claim that the sin of humanity is such an offence against a holy God that the problem is not merely that we do sin, but that we have incurred a debt or a penalty because of that sin. A model which shows how it is possible for us to be brought to repentance and released from sinful behaviour into freedom of life is not enough. There remains a debt to pay, or a penalty to be imposed, or a punishment to be inflicted. If we were to take this on ourselves, it would mean eternal death. Instead, Jesus took it on himself, in our place, as our substitute, on the cross. All we now need to do is receive the forgiveness that Jesus has made possible.

This view is defended and opposed with equal passion. Some protest, saying that if God is love, then forgiveness is just what God is about. The real offence is to suggest that God can't simply forgive.

It is not quite so straightforward. A mother whose child was murdered may find an image of the perpetrator worshipping in the prison chapel, comforted by God's forgiveness, to be appalling. How can God forgive? *He* isn't the victim. *He* is unharmed.

This is a serious point, and one way through is to see how God's forgiveness can only be through Jesus. Of all responsible victims (i.e. victims possessing the faculty of moral responsibility), Jesus alone can stand before the world as one who was not also an oppressor. Through the world making Jesus to be the only 'pure victim', all the sin of the world was represented. Jesus is therefore the only human being with the absolute right to judge, for the rest of us are compromised by being ourselves under judgement. And God therefore has the right to forgive, because, through Jesus, he is the ultimate victim of all sin.[1]

This is a way to see part of what happens when the vicious circle described in the creation model is broken. Forgiveness can flow when a victim tells me I am forgiven who does not also need forgiveness. Christ was 'raised for our justification', as Paul puts it, because he can now tell me, his persecutor, that I am free. I do not need to justify myself, so I am set free to forgive the other *first*, fearing no condemnation, for I know that ultimately I am forgiven even if the other does not now forgive me in return. Indeed, I must forgive, as Jesus taught, for when I deny forgiveness, I deny the source of all forgiveness, and therefore cannot know myself to be forgiven. So God's forgiveness of individuals is not a denial of the reality that there is no true reconciliation if it has not been worked out in human relationships – the point felt by the mother above. It is rather the foundation, established in the real world through the human life and death of Jesus, which makes the hope of such reconciliation possible.

This, however, is not what many people mean when they claim that forgiveness is only possible through Jesus paying the debt or penalty. It is claimed that something more is demanded by the holy character of God himself, in order that God is true to himself. This can be expressed in various ways. It may be insisted that all sin deserves punishment, and that on the cross Jesus took the punishment for everyone. It may be said that God's offended honour requires the payment of a satisfaction to make amends. It may be said that something must be presented in order to make propitiation, that is, to turn away God's wrath.

How far may all this be reconciled with the creation model? To say that God is holy is to say that God must remain true to who he is. It does not add anything additional to his character. Since God is love, 'God is holy' simply says 'God is love' again, but louder. God's life is about nothing other than love.

It is because God is like this that the world is like it is. God's purpose is for the world to be holy; true to who God is; making itself true by its own free response. It is therefore because of who God is that it was necessary for Jesus to give his life that creation may be opened to new life. For God to impose his order on the world would be to deny his own freedom. The death of Jesus was therefore necessary for our salvation because the holy character of God required it. In that sense it is therefore possible to say that Jesus provided satisfaction for sins. He did what was necessary for both the world to be saved and for God's honour to be upheld.

It is also possible to say that Christ's death was a propitiation, to turn away God's wrath, but only in the same way that I may say the sun has risen this morning. Nobody corrects me on the latter, because it is understood that I know that the earth has turned, even though from my perspective the sun has risen. Similarly, it should be understood that 'turn away God's wrath' actually means that the world turns itself away from its course of self-destruction. Whether it is helpful to use the word 'propitiation' is another matter, but it is good as far as possible to seek the truth in language which has served generations.

Again, just as it is possible to say that Jesus 'paid the price' as long as it is understood to be a metaphor, so we can say that the cross was a penalty or a punishment, in the impersonal sense of being a consequence of sin; in the way in which we may speak of tiredness as the penalty or punishment for a late night. Through his obedience, Jesus is drawn into the depths of the world's chaos, and in that place of suffering he remains faithful, thereby opening creation to God. We may therefore also say that here Jesus is our substitute, 'because he does for us what we cannot do for ourselves'.[2]

As the hymn puts it: 'There was no other good enough to pay the price of sin; He only could unlock the gate of heaven and let us in.' It is the gate to the freedom of God, but it could only be opened from within creation, for that is the side on which it was bolted.

However, I do not believe we can say that God inflicted punishment on Jesus – the New Testament does not support this notion. God cannot *inflict* blessing on the world, never mind punishment. It is because of God's holiness that he cannot impose punishment. He cannot but let creation make itself because of his own freedom. And where does the principle come from that all sin must be punished in retribution? We do not apply it in normal human relationships. Even less acceptable is the notion that punishment can be transferred. How can it be just to punish an innocent person? We may admire an innocent person who stands in and takes a beating for another, but we cannot admire the one who administers it. Even if we construe the cross as God punishing himself, it can make no moral sense. Similarly, we cannot speak of wrath as a state in God which needed to be assuaged by an offering, without dishonour to his name. Each of these ways of speaking adds an extra principle to God which is both incomprehensible and incompatible with his love. And a consequence of these explanations is that they transfer the real problem of sin away from the world of human relationships. They originate from a right instinct that forgiveness cannot come cheaply, merely by a word from God, but they leave out what was taught in the Lord's Prayer, that forgiveness from God cannot be separated from forgiveness between each other. The cost of Christ's death was necessary, not to save us from all cost, but to enable the Holy Spirit to lead us into the slow, painful process of forgiveness and reconciliation in the world.

Having said that, from surveying the different approaches above, it is clear that they each express some truth. Also, while none is sufficient in itself, in general they are not mutually exclusive. The attraction of the creation model, I suggest, is that it holds so much together. It does not compromise the self-giving life of God. It enables creation and salvation to be seen together as one. (If God is thought to work in different ways at different times or with different peoples, it suggests an inconsistency which threatens his integrity.) It gives key significance to each aspect of the life of Jesus: incarnation, ministry, death, resurrection, ascension and Pentecost. And it acknowledges the seriousness of sin and evil, for the cross is understood to make a crucial change to the order of the world, in a way which remains mysterious because of our limited perspective yet conceivable because of our knowledge of the integrity of creation. Or to put it another way, the creation model does not offer a worked out solution to the question of the atonement, as if we can stand on ground which allows us to attempt such an exercise. It simply trusts that, if the self-offering of Christ makes the difference, creation must be ordered such that self-offering makes a difference.

11 The Holy Trinity

As we saw earlier, it *may* have been possible to go a long way towards understanding God as Trinity, as one God in three persons, just by reflection and enough reason to trust. Needless to say, that is not how it did happen, even though the Old Testament, with hindsight, can be seen to have pointers in that direction. Rather, through Jesus Christ there came both the reason to trust and the revelation itself.

For Christians, Jesus Christ is the beginning and the end of revelation. He is the beginning because everything that was previously known is now seen to be the beginning of a revelation of him, from the very first sense of God's address by his word. He is the end, not because we now have all facts and understanding – far from it. Rather, we now know that, in Jesus Christ, what God has spoken is *himself*, and therefore he has nothing more to say.

From the New Testament we do not get a sense that the first Christians focused on conjecture and philosophy to work out what difference Jesus must make to their understanding of God. Instead, they recounted the events of the life of Jesus in their worship, witnessed the response of others to the good news, and experienced what could only be described as a new life. And we find that, just as from the earliest writings onwards Jesus is placed alongside God as creator, so the Spirit is called the Holy Spirit. The Spirit is 'Holy' because through him people can have life which is true to who God is, the life of the Son with the Father. How can this Holy One, who makes Jesus more present than when he was present, not also be God?

The Church did not work out the truth, then believe it, then experience the blessing of it. Everything grew together. Life in God cannot be divided up easily. They found themselves knowing God in a new way as Father, as

Jesus knew him. They found themselves knowing each other in a new way, through the gifts of service they were able to offer, and through the love and fellowship they could share. They found themselves knowing hope in a new way, even in the midst of suffering and persecution.

It was therefore by the Spirit that they came to recognize the Spirit. They did not first work out that there must be another in God as well as Father and Son, one who can break the 'unvicious circle' of mutual self-absorption. They did not conclude through theological speculation that God's life must be a giving away such that 'when the Son loves the Father, *he loves one who loves another* . . . [he] doesn't simply love in a reciprocal, mirroring way, but loves the Father who breathes out the Spirit'.[1]

We can now appreciate these wonderful insights, but they first knew themselves as *loved others*, as a people on whom had been poured out the life and love of the Son, who thereby came to see the glory of the life of God the Father, Son and Holy Spirit who loved them.

It is of course not quite so easy to recognize the Spirit as personal, for 'Spirit' does not indicate any relation, and we never hear the Spirit. As noted earlier, the Spirit's work is not to speak but to draw creation forwards by enabling the Word to be heard. The Spirit between us does not speak for us but allows us our true voice. This reticence of the Spirit is necessary for our freedom, so that the Word does not compel, and so that it is truly *our* response. So there is a case for being cautious about using 'he' for the Spirit. To use 'it' is not as inappropriate as sometimes claimed, for we never hear the Spirit use 'I'.

The Spirit is not even a 'force' in the world, and certainly does not *possess* us. In fact, the more effective the Spirit is in our lives, the more we become our true selves. In the same way that God as the ground of the world does not intrude, so the Spirit is not present in the world acting on things as another influence alongside all others. The 'power' of the Spirit is in the response which is enabled when the eyes of one are opened to the challenge or encouragement of another, or when the Word is brought to bear on our lives, or when any part of creation opens to something new.

We speak of the Spirit as a person, even though it seems difficult, because Father, Son and Holy Spirit are co-equal. Yet it is not entirely straightforward to speak of the Father and Son as persons. If we think of Father, Son and Holy Spirit as three persons like ourselves, as three separate individuals with independent minds, then we are far from the unity of God. On the other hand, we cannot think of God as someone who merely acts in three ways or reveals himself in three ways. We are limited by language, and 'person' is the best we can do. As Augustine said, '... they are certainly three ... Yet when you ask "Three what?", human speech labours under a great dearth of words. So we say three persons, not in order to say that precisely, but in order not to be reduced to silence.'[2]

God escapes our categories of thought and speech. We know singular and plural, but here is a unity which is greater than one and a plurality that is not greater than one. The greatest unity is not isolation or sameness, and the greatest plurality is not division or conflict.[3]

We are also at a limit when we say that the Son is begotten of the Father. We use a word which normally implies that one came before the other, but we have no better word. And when the creed says that the Holy Spirit 'proceeds from the Father and the Son', we use the word 'proceeds', not because we know precisely what we are saying, but to distinguish it from 'begotten'.

As we saw earlier, a most important distinction between the persons of the Trinity and ourselves as individuals is that the Father, the Son and the Holy Spirit have their being only in the relationships in which each is held. The relationships constitute the persons; the persons do not *have* relationships. So there is no sequence which orders the Trinity – the independent Father first begetting the Son who is second, with the Spirit proceeding third. The Son is begotten of the Father. In response, the Father is reflected by the Son. The Spirit proceeds from the Father and the Son, while also enabling the relationship between the Father and the Son. Only in these actions together do the Father, Son and Holy Spirit have their being. It is these actions, or this act, which together *is* the being of God as love. God is this eternal love, without beginning or end.

To think of God in this way is continuous with Jesus' understanding of himself as the Son without any remainder to his being. In human relationships, to be a son is just one thing that may be true about a person. For Jesus, there was nothing that he did which was not the Son's response to the Father.

Another way to express this is to say that God's being is identical with his action, the classic understanding of God in Christian thinking. It goes together with the earlier consideration that God is not an object and has no environment. God is this love, a love which overflows in the creation of the world. But there is nothing – no *thing* – in God which can be acted on by the world. The world can respond to God, but it does not determine his action or change him. Therefore, God's action towards the world is wholly for the world's sake, and not for any benefit to God.

In modern times many have recoiled from this conception of a God who appears to be an austere, inert, unmovable power. To be 'without body, parts or *passions*'[4] seems remote and unloving to people today. But there are two reasons why I may be unmoved when, for example, faced with a child suffering from cancer. One is that I am indeed cold and selfish. The other is that I am the child's mother, there 24 hours a day, not needing to be moved because already moved, because the love is constantly in action. Authentic love is not measured by emotional change in the lover but by the response towards the loved. In a far deeper way God is 'already moved'.

To speak of God as unconditioned by the world is a positive, not a negative. It is to say that God always gets his 'response' in first, for his action is always ahead of us. He is unchanged by us, 'without passions', not because he is cold, but because he is so passionate that he could not be more so.[5] God's love never needs to be aroused. Whatever the world becomes, God is the love that it needs.

If God really is changed by us, then it means he in some sense shares our environment and therefore acts on us and is acted on by us in the world as another player. He must in some way be an object, and we may reasonably wonder why he seems unable to demonstrate his existence to us as incontrovertibly as that of other objects. All apart from the fact that it undermines our freedom, for we are then the means by which he becomes what he wills himself to be. Because creation as a whole no longer exists for its own sake, there is no principle which may prevent one part from being possessed by another part as a means to an end.

It may be objected that the Bible speaks of God in our terms, as an actor in the world, especially in the Old Testament. A degree of metaphor and imagery is not contradictory, of course, but there is the more significant question of how to read the Bible's description of God's action which will be discussed later.

We must remember that ultimately it is through Jesus Christ that we know God in this way. As has been noted, it is because God's being is *not* like ours that the incarnation is possible. If we wish to see the agony and vulnerability of God, we do not need to project it onto his eternal being, for we see it in God through the human face of Christ. And while God's being is indeed *other* than ours, the truth of Jesus is that God's life as Father, Son and Holy Spirit is what we are invited into to share. What does that say about the way we are made?

12 Why the Church?

We are now back where we started. Through Jesus it has been revealed that God *is* love, and we are called to share in that life. Is there any more to say? Why not stay with this simple message and resolve to put it into practice? Why complicate it with religion? If we are not here to serve God's interests, or any purpose, why do we need the Church? I can decide to be unselfish and try my best to keep to that in each situation. I can give thanks to God on my own, naturally, at times when I am conscious of the wonder of life.

This is a way of thinking which assumes that we make progress as individuals by first learning about the right way, then deciding to agree to it, and then deciding to act on it. Progress is made as a society when enough people progress on their own as individuals. The engine of improvement for society is the individual, and the engine of improvement for the individual is the will.

We think this is the solution and yet it is the problem that we think like this. We see a feat of will as the answer, when seeing ourselves as feats of will is just what we should question. This is so deeply rooted that the Church can often live by it even though it is founded against it.

It is commonly said that the sin of Adam was that he wanted to be like God, but as we have seen, God's purpose really is that we should be like him. Where Adam went wrong was in thinking that to be God, to have the highest form of life, was to be independent and autonomous, and in making a bid for this 'freedom' he became a slave to dust.

It is a story repeated in each one of us. John Zizioulas puts it in the most extreme form when he strikingly describes a youth in adolescence who asks, 'And who consulted me when I was brought into the world?'[1]

We grow up to realize that there is more to us than being someone's son, daughter, brother or sister. And in reaction we are inclined to imagine, and much of society tells us, that the path to maturity and fulfilment lies in detachment and self-sufficiency. Our identity and security are found by establishing walls of our choice. Our strength is found in being free to choose who we listen to.

Far from growing up, this is an attempt to replace parental security with another kind of protection from the real world – a blanket of wealth or power. Along with the kind of religion which imagines God to be holding us on baby reins, it is a refusal to respond to his call, or push, into adulthood, to accept our existence as material beings given over to the world. It is a failure to recognize that we are made in the image of a God whose essence is interdependence and self-giving.

Underlying this delusion is a perception of ourselves as essentially free agents. There are material limits on our actions imposed by our health and wealth, for example. But in choosing within those constraints we are completely free. We perceive the world, analyze the range of possible options, and decide what to do.

The truth, however, is that our options are limited by the kind of people we have become. This is no less true now than when we were infants. We never just decided to love. We were loved and thereby made capable of loving. We never just decided to speak. We were spoken to and thereby made capable of speaking. Not that we were born as completely blank slates, but based on that innate nature, what we have since become is certainly not simply a result of our decisions.

It is illusory to imagine that all our actions are the result of conscious decision and deliberation. We respond to people and circumstances according to the character of person we are. That is not to say our behaviour is strictly determined, but that there are things we are capable and not capable of. Do we not 'find ourselves' doing things? If we are honest, do we not fear how we may react under certain pressures or threats? And even with actions for which we have time for prior reflection, the scope of our reflection is limited by who we are.

We recognize that the abuse of children inhibits their capacity to love and trust, and we should not imagine that living in an imperfect world leaves any of us without limits on our freedom to respond faithfully to others. This is not to say that we have all been damaged, but that we have not yet been formed. Just as the only way God can make a world is patiently, over time, so we can only *grow* towards the fullness of God's life. It is not about instantly making right decisions, but slowly becoming right people.

Even if we know what a right decision is, we don't necessarily want to take it. We can have free will, yet be aware of our limitations. Augustine said, 'Often we see what we should do but do it not, because the doing does not delight us; and we desire that it may delight us'.[2] How can we make ourselves delight in something that does not attract us?

Far from a negative view of human nature, this is a recognition that there is potential for us to become much more than we are now. The view of Pelagius, whom Augustine opposed, and of many today, is that we are essentially free already. With sufficient effort we can build a community of love. Augustine, on the other hand, believed that freedom is what we will know when we have become a community of love.

We are not free people who must simply learn how to use that freedom in order to get on with each other. Like children, we are people who need others to love us and address us that we may grow into greater freedom, that we may learn to love and speak more faithfully. This is to restate our need of help from beyond ourselves. We are in a circle where we need to set each other free, yet none of us is free to offer freedom.

This is why the gospel of Christ is so much more than a teaching about love. It is the gift of love itself, by the Holy Spirit, to whom the world has been opened by Christ. As Paul writes, 'God's love has been poured into our hearts through the Holy Spirit that has been given to us' (Romans 5.5). And the gift of 'God's love' is not so much an awareness that we are loved by God, but the ability to love with God's love.

Yet again we could fall into the trap of making this an individual exercise. The Holy Spirit gives to me the gift of love and then I go and put it into practice. We still don't really need the Church because I can pray and read the Bible on my own, and open myself to the Spirit.

But the Spirit can't do this, in just the same way that God can't make a perfect world just by putting together lots of perfect parts. The world is finding its freedom by finding itself. God could not teach me to speak without my parents, and God cannot make me Christian without the Church. If we do not really need others in order to grow to maturity, then for exactly the same reason we never needed Christ.

We are prone to see others as a threat to our freedom, where love is the answer to how we may live together without destroying each other. This is the negative view of human nature. The Christian way is to see others as the path to our freedom, and love is the answer to how we may create each other by living together.

Hell does not lie in 'other people' but the isolated self. Those who close off open, creative communication with the world do not become free, but slaves to their own internal desires. Possibly the only free actions we make are when we give of ourselves; everything else is a kind of animal instinct.

John wrote, 'Beloved, we are God's children now; what we will be has not yet been revealed' (1 John 3.2). The Christian hope is for something far more wonderful than success in making the right decisions. Through our openness to others we make it possible for us to become something we could never imagine, let alone decide, for ourselves. God *is* his love, in a fuller way than we could ever be. But we should not have expected that our love for each other would be altogether an extra to the formation of our being. In a profound sense it is the making of us.

It therefore follows that belief in the God of Jesus Christ could never have been a private affair. To believe in God who is Father, Son and Holy Spirit is to be together in order to receive and share that life. This is the Church.

13 The Church

God's life is gratuitous self-giving and response; the whole world is called to share in this life; Jesus has opened the way for us to know such life together by the Spirit. This is what the Church believes, and the Church exists because when we are open to each other we become open to God, and when we are open to God we become open to each other. At the same time, the Church must be open to the world, because the whole creation is to be made free, and that can only happen together. It is no more possible for the Church to be brought to wholeness in isolation than for an individual.

So the Church is marked by openness to God, openness to others, and openness to the world. We will consider the life of the Church under these headings in order to give a framework, not because they are really separable. The Nicene Creed speaks of one 'holy, catholic and apostolic' Church, which corresponds roughly with 'God, others and the world', but unless all are true, none is true.

The Church is open to God because it is his life that everything is about, and his life that it seeks. The life it now knows is not what it could be or should be, so it is constantly repentant, aware that it needs to be transformed. Reminding itself of God's holiness, the Church recognizes its need. This can easily be misunderstood as an unhealthy and negative attitude, for is it not affirmation that we need if we are to grow?

The Gospels contain the remarkable story of a sick woman who is thereby 'unclean' according to the law. She touches Jesus without him knowing, and instead of Jesus being made 'unclean', as would have been expected, she is healed. This illustrates that it is precisely because Jesus is holy that those who come to him are made whole. He is unchangingly true to who he is, so it is the other who is transformed.

God's holiness is the source of our joy and renewing. We can confidently come together as a Church without pretence or denial, acknowledging honestly our lack of health. Because God is holy, nothing can change him from being who he is. He cannot love us less, and he certainly does not need to withdraw from us in order to protect his purity. By making herself present and open to God, the Church can be healed and affirmed. The good news we wish to hear from the doctor is not the list of body parts that are well but hope that the diseased part can be cured. The affirmation we need to hear from God is not a positive appraisal on what is good, but hope that nothing is beyond forgiveness and healing.

That is why repentance goes together with faith in Jesus Christ. Through him, nothing is now held back from becoming free. As the Church gathers together, it opens itself to God by hearing the story of his saving action in the world through Jesus. Faith is thereby encouraged, and the people have confidence to draw near to God with what the *Book of Common Prayer* calls 'hearty repentance', helpfully suggesting a manner that is both sincere and spirited.

And spirited it is, for as we shall see later, in the one Spirit each member was baptized on becoming a member of the Church, and in that one Spirit the Church lives. In the Church, as it is open to God, the Spirit does what the Spirit always does: enables the Word to be heard and received, and enables self-giving in response. This receiving of gift and becoming gift reaches its highest in the Church's most central act of worship, the Eucharist, which again we shall consider later.

In the worship of the Church therefore, we see all different aspects of giving and receiving weave together: repentance, faith, hearing, thanksgiving and praise. The Church receives healing from God, and offers praise to God. And in among all that there is to be joy. Worship is not only a purposeful receiving of life and a dutiful giving of thanks, but a pointless delighting in God. I do not pause to view the sunrise because I think it is good for me, or because I feel I ought to. I do it because I am taken out of myself in wonder. The Church's openness to God should have a similar note of freedom.

In spite of the fact that the Church always needs to repent, we call it 'holy'. That is not a claim regarding the way of life of its members, for they are clearly not unfailingly true to who God is. The Church's holiness derives from the fact that it is formed, not merely by people associating with each other, but by each being united with Christ by the Spirit. The Lord of the Church is bound inseparably to its members. What is it that is unchangingly true to God about the Church? It is the Church of *Christ*. The Church is therefore holy, and the New Testament speaks of its individual members as holy people, or saints.

For the same reason, the Church is 'one'. Since all Christians are joined to Christ, they are joined to each other. Through the Spirit, God himself is one, and as we have seen, the Spirit is present in all creation, drawing everything to respond to the other in order to build integrity. Through Christ, the Church's task is to express this unity as a sign of God's purpose for the world to be made whole.

The Church is therefore a community where each must seek to be open to the other. The New Testament uses the image of a body, the body of Christ, where every member is linked together, and each needs the other in order to find health. This is applied in relation to the variety of gifts which the members have. These are not talents to be held in possession, but the means by which we may give ourselves. Whether it is practical care, teaching the community, or miracles of healing, the gift is given that each may become a gift.

This may be most obvious in a local church, but an openness to what the other has to give knows no boundaries in space or time. The Church is therefore a 'communion of saints' which holds together both the living and the departed. And while the Spirit always draws us to the future, it is the same Spirit who connects us with the past, to give attention to the tradition which has been handed down. The Spirit's work is not to inspire novelty *per se*. Without an openness to the past we would have no faith that the future will be made new.

Of particular importance within the Church's tradition is the Bible, to the point that we often speak of Scripture and tradition as if they were separate. We will consider later how these writings are an essential means by which we may become open to God and to each other. But the teachings and practices of the Church throughout all the centuries are neglected at our cost, as are the lives of those saints who have become examples of what is possible in the freedom of the Spirit. History is not uniform progress, and the Church often needs to recover its memory.

This is all part of the Church's crucial work of repentance and a constant reminder that Christ's likeness has yet to be wholly formed in her life. The Word has not yet been fully heard and we cannot be closed to any voice. No one possesses the whole truth, yet everyone is a truth to be heard by the whole Church. The ordering of the Church's life must always express this. The individual must not be sacrificed for the sake of a monolithic body, nor the body sacrificed for the sake of individual autonomy. Here is the heart of the Church's life, not just as a means to its growth, but as the expression of its gratuitous freedom.

The most fundamental order in the Church is baptism, by which each is made a part of the body. In New Testament terms the whole Church is a priesthood, so baptism may be described as an ordination. Every member is a priest, for by virtue of their baptism alone they are called to offer the sacrifice of themselves. The historic orders of bishop, priest (in a different sense) and deacon are not clearly laid out in the New Testament, but as Archbishop Michael Ramsey said, the point is not to be archaeological but evangelical.[1]

What matters is not that the order should model precisely what was practised by the first Christians (a mixed and developing picture anyway) but that it should reflect the gospel.

The key to the threefold order is the bishop. By this episcopacy, or oversight, the unity of the Church is expressed, both by linking each congregation with the whole and by a visible dependence on the historic Church and its apostles. In their ministry, the priests and deacons, who have been ordained by the bishop, make the wider body visible to the local church and make the local church to be a visible expression of the whole body. That any ordination (including baptism) is not possible without the whole body is properly expressed by the presence of the wider community. Far from being lifeless institutionalism, the orders of ministry are therefore an openness to the Spirit, that the Church may express the truth that no part of it will come to full maturity in Christ apart from the whole body.

It is therefore important to recognize that the orders of ministry exist to enable the Church to listen to itself rather than to control what is heard. As part of that, the clergy have a key role in handing on what has been handed down. But their gifts of oversight, pastoring and teaching are there to allow the freedom of the Spirit that each may become a gift to the other. So paradoxically it is the ordering itself that allows space for the disturbing, awkward, prophetic voice.

This profound belief in the Church as a whole is an important part of the meaning of the word 'catholic', but beyond that it describes an openness to all humanity and the world. The early Christians came to see that the good news was not just for the Jews but for all peoples. In the Church, says Paul, 'There is no longer Jew or Greek, there is no longer slave or free, there is no longer male and female; for all of you are one in Christ Jesus' (Galatians 3.28). The Church exists for everybody because it exists for no group in particular.[2]

More than that, the Church is catholic in its concern with all of human life and creation. The reason the Church is only a part of the world and only does particular things is not because God sees any divide between what is sacred and secular, or between what is spiritual and material. The Church's membership does not represent that limited part of the world which belongs to God, nor does its worship represent that limited activity which matters to God. Unlike the Inland Revenue, God is not another body alongside everything else in creation, interested in only one aspect of us, needing something from us, and occupying a part of our time in providing it. Nor is God only a part like oxygen, as that which we depend on – present at all times, acknowledged by our breathing, but of no meaning for the rest of life.

God's life is the music to which everything in creation is called to dance. Our whole world is to be an expression of God's life in a different form. It is not without significance that the shift in scientific understanding of the most basic elements of matter, which we have already noted, has been away from the rigidity of a mechanism towards the freedom of a dance. God's purpose is that by his Word and Spirit this music should be the shape of our being. The Church's role is to enable the tune of God's self-giving love to be heard and to bring hope that the dance is possible. In this the Church is catholic, for it is about the whole of life; and it is apostolic, for this is good news to live and proclaim.

The Church's life is far from being the whole dance. In its worship, the Church listens that the music may form its being, and it is set free to dance. It therefore becomes an effective sign or sacrament of God's life, but without being able to dictate how the world should move, and without any competition for space. The Church is not the only player on the stage, nor is it the world's choreographer; it doesn't even know all the moves.

It is the hard truth that throughout history the Church has often been no less ungainly than the rest of the world, to put it euphemistically, and today much of its performance is graceless. The gap between the real Church and the ideal described in this chapter hardly needs to be mentioned. But for all that, there are past and present examples of attractive social movement and costly individual sacrifice which live out the tune and inspire hope. If the Church's credibility depended on its overall greater goodness and success, then we may despair. But its ability to bear witness to the hope of freedom comes by its way of repentance and examples of holiness.

The Christian faith was not founded on success. No matter the manner in which the Church is broken, whether through failure, or persecution, or the pain which may afflict any part of humanity, it remains the body of Christ, and its sufferings are his. In the light of the cross everything looks different. Weakness, foolishness and shame are the path to strength, wisdom and glory. Only by sharing in Christ's suffering is it possible to share in his victory. The Church does not look for martyrdom, and cannot rest in failure, but it knows that it is not reliant on its own achievements or resources.

The Church has no *plan* to save itself, never mind to save the world. Its message is not a programme for survival or a system of solutions to global problems. It is the way of Christ crucified. It is a call to find life by losing it. It is about an openness to the other, that the Spirit may give us awareness and teach us how to live as gifts. In practice this may often look more like failure. It is certainly not about always being right. Often the Church has needed to learn from the world, in areas where it should have known better, such as the freedom of women. Far from being a compromise, to admit this is true to the Church's message of openness. The Spirit is present in the whole world, and light may come from the most unexpected source. The philosopher Nietzsche said that the Church would have to look more saved before he could believe in its Saviour, but it could be argued that the world would have to look more godless before we could believe in its Godlessness.

For this reason the Church has a duty to be in dialogue with people of other faiths and none, whose insights it may sometimes need. And more, while confident that God's life as expressed in Jesus is something for all humanity, without any contradiction it should not live by defending and expanding a domain. For the essence of this life is the freedom grounded in the God of Jesus Christ that no human organization, and not even God, should be a dominating presence. Or rather, the Church does proclaim 'Jesus is *Lord*' (Latin *Dominus*), but knowing that he redefined lordship as washing feet. Therefore, when the Church is true to its head, any privileged place which it may have in public life is marked by a hospitality to others which stems from having no interest in protecting either itself or God. The Church is then able to be an effective sign of the freedom of God, without which life is never more than a struggle between competing interests.

14 Baptism

We shall now consider some of the practices of the Church in more detail, beginning with baptism. From the start this was the rite of initiation as a follower of Christ, and according to the very end of Matthew's Gospel, it is based on a command from Jesus himself:

> Go therefore and make disciples of all nations, baptizing them in the name of the Father and of the Son and of the Holy Spirit, and teaching them to obey everything that I have commanded you. And remember, I am with you always, to the end of the age. (Matthew 28.19f.)

It is notable that the command to baptize sits alongside the promise of the presence of Jesus, for the essence of baptism is to be placed with Jesus. John the Baptist arrived preaching repentance and baptizing in the river Jordan. This was both new and prophetic, though the washing may have some continuity with Jewish ritual cleansings of the time. As we have seen, Jesus was baptized by John at the beginning of his ministry, when he was declared to be the Son as the Spirit descended upon him. Later, as Jesus moves with his disciples towards Jerusalem, he speaks of his own suffering and death as a baptism, a baptism in which they would come to share.

The New Testament uses a number of images to describe baptism, including burial and resurrection. Christian baptism is baptism 'into Christ Jesus'. It is to be buried with him in his death in order that we may share in his risen life. That is why full immersion in water is a particularly vivid mode of baptism. But what does it mean?

We have seen from the beginning of creation that water is a symbol of the chaos from which order is drawn by God's Word and the hovering Spirit. The same image is present in relation to the deliverance of the people of Israel from slavery through the waters of the Red Sea, parted by a wind from God. Similarly, the baptism of Jesus symbolizes him entering the disorder of this world by the strength of the Holy Spirit, emphasized in the Gospels by being followed immediately by his temptation by the devil in the desert for 40 days. The whole ministry of Jesus is a deepening of his baptism, culminating in the baptism of his death, when he enters the deepest waters, engulfed by the chaotic self-destructive forces of creation. And by this act of self-giving the door was opened to new life for the world.

To be baptized as a Christian is to be so united with Jesus by the Spirit that what happened to Jesus can happen to us. We have seen that the whole benefit of what Jesus has done lies in the opening of creation to the renewing of the Spirit. The world is not yet free from chaos, and we ourselves are a part of that disorder. In baptism we are joined with Christ, and thereby with the Church which is his body. We are immersed in him, as it were, into a place where all that is selfish in us can be put to death and from where new life can be drawn.

The Church baptizes believing that God can work. Baptism is an act of faith. It is not a mechanical or magical means of dispensing grace or of influencing God. In baptism, God is acting as he always does: making the world what it makes itself to be by its response. Here is a physical act with water, in accordance with the command of Christ and the practice of the Church down the centuries, accompanied by confidence in all that has been made possible through Jesus. It is not merely a symbol or an aid to the visualization of a truth. It is a sacrament in that it is effective towards that which it signifies.

Baptism would make no sense without an understanding of the work of the Spirit in creation. The Church brings us to the water trusting that the Spirit broods overhead. Placed in the water with Jesus, the Spirit is able to make a difference. This is not where we come to full maturity, but it is a beginning of life. Having entered into Christ's death, it is possible to go on with the daily work of dying to self that we may be raised to new life. Having come to new birth, to use another New Testament image, that life can be expected to grow. Having been placed at the source of forgiveness in Jesus, where sins can be washed away, it is possible to work that out in the body where forgiveness is given and received mutually.

All these different images have in common the truth that how we are is not how we have to remain. This is the way things have been from the beginning of creation. The Spirit constantly draws the world forwards, that its response may make it possible for everything to be brought to greater freedom. Jesus has opened creation to the future, overcoming the force whereby we held each other down, and now in baptism we are placed where our self-giving response may be released by being united with him.

Baptism happens once but is never left behind. We are always on our way out of the water. Jesus said, 'If anyone would come after me, let him deny himself, take up his cross daily and follow me.' We are in a new place with Jesus, but Good Friday and Easter are to be the shape of our lives. We know God as Jesus did, addressing him as 'Our Father', but for us that is a daily prayer that we may be forgiven as we forgive one another. We may be on the far side of the Red Sea, but we have not yet crossed the desert to the promised land.

On coming through the water we do not find ourselves removed from this world, but assured within it by the Spirit that, if we follow in the way of the cross, we will also share in the way of resurrection life. So our Easter life is not about the maintenance of an unremitting note of triumph. It gives us confidence to die to ourselves. It helps us not to fear the painful ordering of our unruly wills and affections. It helps me to trust that the death of my selfishness will not be the death of myself.

The New Testament places great emphasis on the task of progression and the danger of regression. Our salvation is something we need to work out as God works in us. It is for this reason that arguments about precisely when or where we are 'saved' are futile, particularly when 'saved' is interpreted narrowly as an individual escape from hell and entrance into heaven in the next life. It is as unnecessary to belittle the effectiveness of either a conversion experience or baptism as it is unhelpful to insist that either are where it all happens. In the full picture, 'salvation' is the whole work of creation, and this is reflected in the broad and flexible use of such language in the Bible.

So while I have argued that it is a contradiction to be alone as a follower of Jesus, outside of baptism and the Church, at the same time it cannot be claimed that no salvation is happening outside of the Church. Ultimately, the world will only be saved together, and through Christ, but the Spirit is not so limited that any who spend their whole lives outside of the Church must be for ever lost. The Church belongs to Christ, but Christ is not the property of the Church.

Because the Spirit's work is not limited to those who have a conscious Christian faith, and for a variety of other reasons, it may be considered proper to baptize infants. It is true that the New Testament says nothing explicit about infant baptism, and that little is known of the practice of the Church in its first years, but the settled conclusion of the greater part of the Church from the early centuries onwards has been in favour.

The physical act of baptism must be accompanied by faith, and a responsible candidate must clearly have a degree of faith in order to come to that decision, but the wider faith of the Church must be recognized, and that of parents and godparents in the case of infants. Once the emphasis is put on the faith of the candidate, we may ask precisely how much faith is required.

Baptism has here been described as the beginning, not as a stage of maturity in understanding or faith. It is about being placed in a new environment in order that faith can grow, not because faith has grown. It is a recognition that without being together with each other in Christ, we are floundering on our own. It comes back again to the reason why we need the Church in the first place: because our growth is not possible by a feat of will as individuals. Put like that, Christian parents may consider the baptism of their children to be rather necessary.

Can children be excluded from the Church, of whom Jesus said 'to such belongs the kingdom of God'? It appears that Jesus uses children as an example of how to receive the kingdom because their sense of dependence means that they are more naturally open, more able to accept a gift. Since the very goal of creation is that we may be open to each other as gifts, it would seem strange to have to deny entrance to those who exemplify that.

It is this openness that removes any boundaries from the catholic Church, for God's concern is for the whole world to become one. That there should be 'no longer young or old' is therefore a natural extension of 'no longer Jew or Greek' or 'no longer male or female'. Each part needs the other, so children have an important place in the Church, not just for their benefit, but because their presence is a creative word which calls for a response. They help the whole Church to grow in maturity. They are part of the Church's task of making itself by attentiveness to the word from the other.

Jesus said, 'Let the children come to me', and baptism allows precisely that. For infants, as for anybody, baptism is about being placed with Jesus. It is here where we can learn to live God's life, as we know God as Father. In considering the divinity of Jesus I suggested that our personal identity is not found in any quality we have. Jesus is the Son because of his relation to the Father, not because of something special about his humanity. Similarly we may say that baptism is where we learn our identity, for in this place we hear God call us by name. As Paul says, 'When we cry "Abba! Father!" it is that very Spirit bearing witness with our spirit that we are children of God' (Romans 8.16).

15 The Bible

What about the Bible? This is the question which by now may be in the mind of the reader, whether a sceptic or a believer. The sceptic may point out that I am relying on the Bible to build a case for the significance of Jesus, yet it contains some clear historical inaccuracies compared with external evidence, and some internal contradictions between parallel passages. How then can it be trusted?

Both the sceptic and the believer may charge me with ignoring large parts of the Bible. I have argued that God does not share our environment and therefore we cannot see his actions as a sequence of deliberate and particular interventions to plan and direct events. Rather, by his Word and Spirit, God gives creation freedom, and over time he draws it forwards in response. Yet much of the Old Testament is the story of a world where God is a player who intervenes in the detail, rewarding the good and punishing the wicked.

For the sceptic, this is just further evidence that religion is man-made, and therefore untrustworthy, for I seem to be selective about the parts of the Bible which I use, conveniently ignoring anything which portrays God less attractively. The believer also criticizes my theology for being a human invention, instead of being guided by the plain sense of the whole of God-given Scripture, no matter how hard that may be to hear.

These different viewpoints raise the same basic question: What kind of book is the Bible? To Christians it is special, even holy, but what does that mean? To begin to answer this, it is necessary to consider its origins.

The books of the Bible were written by many authors over hundreds of years; the New Testament in a much shorter period, considerably closer to the events described. In the case of each Testament, even after all the books had been written, there was a period during which the content of the 'Canon' (the approved list of books for use in the community of faith) was being decided. So both the people of Israel and the Church existed long before their Bible existed. They were not without *anything* for all the time before the Canon was settled, but they did not have a fixed collection of writings with a clear boundary.

So neither Judaism nor Christianity are faiths which began with a book. The Church did not form around an authoritative text which people believed had dropped from heaven. The faith came first because people experienced what they understood to be God's salvation. The Bible is written testimony to God's acts, and to the experience of the people of faith.

So Christian faith is not founded on a prior belief about the reliability of the Bible. The contents of the Bible were agreed on the basis of whether or not they were true to the faith of the community. Of course, as they were written, there was a two-way process, as the books both reflected and formed that faith. It came to be recognized that in some way God had been at work in the writing, even giving something new, but it was the significance of the content that led to a conclusion about the origin, not vice versa.

The Bible is therefore indispensable for the Church as that unique collection of writings, brought together over centuries, which bears witness to Christ. It gives us the history of the people through whom he came, the events of his life, and the experience of the early years of his followers. The Church's belief rests on Jesus Christ, in whom God has revealed himself, and without the Bible we would be cut off from this good news. The Christian faith is not a theory or an ethic derived from timeless principles. It is based on events in history, including its Jewish origins, and for that reason a record of those events needed to be written and handed down, largely in narrative form.

But the Church has never regarded the Bible as merely an archive to be critically assessed. If this is the record of where God's salvation has been at work, where the Spirit has been able to draw creation forwards, then these writings are born from the people at the heart of that action. The Spirit's work was evident not just in Jesus himself, but in the life of the early Church, in the writers of the books who both shaped and were shaped by the Church, and in the process of discernment of the Canon by the Fathers of the Church.

The Bible is therefore not just a record of God's salvation. Its production was itself a part of that process of salvation, and its place in the

Church is now necessary as a means to salvation. To say all this is to recognize the Spirit's prompting at each stage. The Bible can therefore be the bearer of good news now, when through the Spirit the text becomes the means by which the Word is heard.

The unique place of the Bible in the life of the Church therefore derives from the Spirit. One of the New Testament letters explicitly states that 'All scripture is inspired by God' (2 Timothy 3.16). But we should note this still does not claim that the Bible is in any sense written directly by God. As we have seen, the Spirit is active in the whole of creation, and all manner of activities may be spoken of as 'inspired'. It is a term we commonly use in relation to the arts, and we certainly cannot deny the Spirit's activity there. For the reasons given, the Church cannot regard the Bible as on the same level as Shakespeare, but at the same time, to speak of it as inspired does not set it apart as produced by an altogether different process from any other writing. It is worth noting that Scripture is described as 'inspired by God' in order to make the rather modest point that it is 'useful'.

However, some Christians believe that it is necessary to say more. Rarely will it be insisted that the Bible was dictated by God, bypassing the minds of the writers. But many claim that the inspiration was such that the writers were prevented from making any errors in matters of fact (including historical fact) or faith. There are many variations on what is meant by this, but they have in common some kind of claim to infallibility. It is this idea which gives rise to the questions with which I began this chapter. My imaginary believer will not allow anything to be said which challenges any part of the Bible because it is perfect. In response, my imaginary sceptic cannot believe anything in the Bible because it seems not to be perfect.

It needs to be said that the Bible itself does not support the idea of infallibility. Nowhere is this claimed within the text, and on occasion the text raises difficulties suggesting otherwise. Even if we take account of the different genres of writing, there are points of historical inaccuracy or internal contradiction between parallel passages which need to be answered. It is always possible for people to construct an explanation, but it often needs to be tortuous. For example, how many times do we have to make Peter deny Jesus to make the Gospels agree? How many ways did Judas Iscariot die? So if we let the Bible speak for itself, we do not conclude that it is infallible. The awkward rationalizations are made necessary by a prior commitment to the Bible's infallibility.

The same is true when we consider what the Bible says about God. For example, the second book of Kings tells us that after the people of Israel were exiled to Assyria, others came to live in the vacated cities of Samaria and, 'When they first settled there, they did not worship the Lord; therefore the Lord sent lions among them, which killed some of them' (2 Kings 17.25). If we suppose the history to be true, must we believe that God deliberately set out to kill people with lions because they did not worship him? Is this consistent with the God of Jesus Christ? Is this how God acts now? If not, does it make it any more acceptable that he only used to act this way?

And this is far from being an isolated example. My imaginary sceptic will be quick to point out, among other horrors, God's will to 'blot out' (Genesis 6.7) human life from the earth (with the exception of the favoured few) in the story of Noah and the flood, and the slaughter of men, women and children commanded by God in the accounts of Israel's occupation of the land of Canaan. I am not dismissing such passages, or even denying that they are 'inspired' and 'useful' writings, but if we have to take at face value what they say concerning God, we cannot at the same time allow Jesus Christ to be the full revelation of God which the Church believes him to be.

The sceptic may ask for an infallible Bible before believing. The believer may consider it to be an expression of trust in God to accept that he has provided an infallible Bible. But both are asking for a way to short-circuit the business of trusting other people. Each needs a mechanism which gives certainty without relying on failing humans. Yet paradoxically this would make God himself less trustworthy.

Through Jesus Christ we learn of God's utter freedom. God's life is gratuitous self-giving where the other is never used as a means to an end. In creation, God cannot be other than this, therefore we can trust that we do not exist to serve God's interests. Furthermore, we can trust that God will never intervene to override our freedom, even for the benefit of others. We may therefore wonder how it could be possible for God so to use a writer as an instrument, even a willing writer open to the Spirit, that not the slightest fault may occur. And if this did happen, should it not have been relatively simple for God to ensure the avoidance of subsequent transcription errors?

More than that, because of God's freedom, his purpose is that this world should be free. And we can only find that freedom with one another, for if it were imposed by God we would not be free. What freedom we know is what the degree of openness in our relationships with each other has made possible, over the history of the world. We should therefore be alert to the temptation of any offer of freedom which bypasses trust in each other. An infallible Bible seems to do just this. No longer are we really relying on the writers and their faith, or the communities in which they lived, or the history of the people to which they belonged. No longer do we need to rely so much on each other in the Church to understand the Bible, for the surface text is God's direct word, simply accessible to each individual.

My sceptic and believer therefore fall into the same trap. Each needs the truth to be accessible with objective certainty, independent of the subjective witness of other humans, the only difference being that one believes that the Bible provides this, and the other does not. Indeed, perversely, we are all prone to seek the truth without seeking each other, when all the time the truth *is* 'nothing without the other'.[1]

That is the truth of God in Jesus Christ.

Admittedly, this leaves things feeling more messy and less controllable, but that is the way of faith. To wish for an infallible Bible or an infallible Church is to wish away our freedom, for it is to wish away God's freedom by placing him within our grasp. The fear of growing up may lurk again, for the appeal of certainty may lie in the protection it offers from the need for vulnerable engagement with the other.

Yet in accepting that the Bible is fallible we are not denying its significance in the Church. (To grow from naïve security into disregard is not to come to maturity, but to pass from childhood into adolescence.) On the contrary, we are more bound to stay with it, for we cannot simply lift truth off the surface of the page and leave the text behind. We cannot expect to construct a neat system to which the Bible becomes a set of supporting footnotes. The Church should therefore be careful not to attach more importance to talking about the Bible than to reading it together.

'Together' is the crucial element. Of course, it matters that the Bible is read individually, but its interpretation can never be private, nor the possession of an authoritative few. The Church believes that Jesus Christ is the full revelation of God and that through the Bible we may encounter him. But the personal, creative Word is not in our control. It is the Spirit who can make him known, and we are only open to the Spirit inasmuch as we are open to each other.

The Church must therefore look into the whole Bible in order to see God in Jesus Christ. It does this, not with a naïve acceptance (for it can only be read in the light of Christ), nor with a superior criticism (for it never completely knows the light of Christ). This is not always easy, but we are certainly not left in the dark. Both the believer and the sceptic may fear that nothing is sure, but true witness is ultimately self-authenticating, and carries its own power of conviction. It is the gospel itself which can grip our hearts, not a claim about the Bible.

In the Church, we seek to read the Bible in a Christian way with our eyes corrected by the gospel, while at the same time our reading of the Bible is a means by which our eyes are corrected. So we learn to read with discernment, and we find the truth about ourselves discerned. We hear people of faith tell what they see, whether they are standing on a clear peak or whether they have the limited perspective of the forest floor. Sometimes they seem to be in both places at once, and the division is certainly not clear cut between the Old and New Testaments. And it reminds us that we are never above it all ourselves.

The Church therefore continually seeks to understand, just as it continually needs to repent. Sometimes it is considered to cast doubt on the Church's credibility that its thinking develops and changes, but its faith is in the fullness of the revelation of God in Christ, not in the exhaustiveness of a body of doctrine. We need only consider the gradual clarification of the doctrine of the Trinity in the early centuries to see that development was both possible and necessary within the normative boundary of Scripture.

Scripture as a whole, read in the light of Christ, accompanied by the gathered wisdom of the ages and of our own time, may point us to say things which we do not find explicitly in the Bible itself. That is how it has always been, and that is why many have thought it necessary (and not just in modern times) to see that the whole leads us beyond the typical Old Testament picture of God as another player in the world (to pick up on the point made at the end of Chapter 11).[2]

Here was a people who believed that God had been active among them to bring salvation, so to express that they wrote what was inevitably, at that stage in their understanding, a mix of legend and history, as if God stepped in as necessary to save or to judge.

That we cannot now speak of God in this way does not imply that these Scriptures must be discarded, or that the writers simply got it all wrong. One of the tensions in the Old Testament is between the voice which says, 'Do good, and all will go well with you' and the voice which replies, 'I did, and it didn't.'[3]

One tells of a God who intervenes to ensure that the righteous are blessed and the wicked are punished, allowing the corollary that suffering must usually be the result of sin. It is found particularly in the book of Deuteronomy, and in many of the historical narratives. The other highlights the reality of innocent suffering, and is found in the books of Job and Isaiah, and some of the Psalms, for example.

In response to this division, some consider the Christian faith to side wholly with the latter voice. Jesus is the ultimate example of innocent suffering. Having nothing to do with retributive punishment, God shows through the cross that he loves us and shares our pain. This approach is not without appeal, but it struggles to show how Christ overcomes sin and evil.

While I have rejected the idea that God inflicts retributive punishment on individuals, or on Jesus, I have described the world as a place for which we have real responsibility. Its freedom depends on our response. God can only bring it to the degree of glory which our self-giving allows. It is for this reason that Christ makes the difference. Because he did good in his life and in his death, it is possible for all to go well with the world. The principle that our good or evil response takes us forwards to glory or backwards into chaos is written into the fabric of creation by virtue of God's freedom.

Because both voices bear truth, this is a helpful warning against rejecting any part of Scripture. It also illustrates the fact that greater light usually reveals a truth which does not simply expose one side of an argument as right and the other as wrong. This should both save us from arrogance and build us in confidence. If we disagree, we need to read the Bible more, together. We listen to Scripture with openness, asking: What is the gift to me? What is the word to shape me?

The Bible does not put us in control of the last word. It enables us to hear the one who is both the first and last Word. This can seem unsettling, for we never know how we may need to be put right. By definition, we don't know what is in our blind spots. But as the brighter light of judgement shines, it will surely be clear that what we lose was never worth keeping, and what we gain is greater glory.

16 Prayer

Jesus summarized the law in two commandments: 'You shall love the Lord your God with all your heart, and with all your soul, and with all your mind' and 'You shall love your neighbour as yourself' (Matthew 22.37–39). One commandment would not be sufficient, much as we may find it neater. It is tempting to think that it is only God who really matters, and all love of our neighbour is ultimately a means by which we express our love for God. This is the kind of pietism which cannot accept that the world exists for its own sake. On the other hand, it appeals to some to think that it is only our neighbour who really matters, and love of our neighbour *is* love of God. This is the kind of humanism which cannot accept that God exists for his own sake.

Although these two loves are not the same thing, we can hold them together as manifestations of the same kind of life. Both are God's life, into which we are baptized as we are united with Christ. Whether it be with God or our neighbour, the Spirit draws our attentiveness to the other and enables our self-giving response.

Prayer is therefore something we cannot ignore, for it is an essential part of loving God. But at the same time it is not a communication line which we need to set up, for in Christ it is already open. The Spirit teaches us to know God intimately as 'Father', in the same way that Jesus did. This is not an advanced level of Christian prayer that we reach after first beginning with address to a distant potentate. It is the entry level, and the only level, which we know to be possible because of what Jesus has revealed about God.

While we love both God and neighbour, the way we relate to God in prayer is not the same as the way we relate to any other person, for there is no symmetry between our part and God's. God is the cause of our being, so we cannot locate him, or engage his attention, or assess his

93

reaction. If we find ourselves really praying it is because God is holding our being in existence, addressing us, and enabling us to hear and respond. And in all that, while God is never an object to us, he is closer than anything we could ever grasp.

Based on that account of prayer, there is a sense in which all creation at some level 'prays'. Prayer as we normally speak of it is continuous with the response of matter in whatever form, as described earlier. It is therefore something we are made for, of which God's part is already happening. Not that we can neatly separate God's part and ours, but prayer is certainly more about allowing ourselves to be caught up in God's action than to be working up our own.

Since prayer is a natural part of being a creature, it has nothing to do with trying to escape our bodies. It is not about awakening or connecting with a 'spiritual side' of us. There is nothing about us that is not 'spiritual', for all life is enabled by the Spirit. It is the Spirit who enables any response, and in prayer we open our whole selves, and through us, to a degree, the whole creation, that the Spirit may bring us to a fuller life of self-giving.

So prayer is not about a part of our being, as if God only relates to a substance called 'spirit' as distinct from 'matter'. Nor is prayer about a part of our lives, as if our relationship with God were one other in a list of relationships including family and friends. When we pray we use our whole being and we bring our whole lives. We could say that prayer is about consciously making everything about us open before God. To pray is not so much to make a list of desires and praises to offer to God, as to offer to God the list of desires and praises that make us – 'the soul in paraphrase', as the poet George Herbert described it.[1]

In other relationships we may be cautious about what we reveal in order to protect ourselves or impress others, but we should not imagine that our performance in prayer either conceals anything from God or influences his response. To the extent that we are not really honest, we are not really praying. That is why it is dangerous to focus on 'success' in prayer, in the form of an 'uplifting experience', for example, for then we may achieve the goal but not the prayer. To pray is to entrust our whole selves to God without setting the agenda.

That is why it is good to begin with a recognition of our total dependence on God, as in the words of the *Book of Common Prayer*: 'O Lord, open thou our lips.'[2]

Far from needing to rise from our bodies, it is in our bodies that we know God's presence and action, and it is through our existence as bodies that God will enable us to pray. So we do not rush into requests but give time to acknowledge God's work. Our bodies, the place where we are, the others we may be with, all can cease to be distractions if we see that each is dynamically held in God and by God.

In seeing ourselves as set in God's action we must also be reminded that our prayer has only been made possible because of all that God has done through history among people of faith, to whom we belong. It is therefore necessary to read the Scriptures which tell of God's salvation and give us hope that, as we open ourselves to the Spirit in prayer, we may in the same way be drawn nearer to God's life. Prayer is therefore never truly solitary, for we can only ever pray as part of the body of Christ. Even when alone we say, '*Our* Father.'

In this way we seek to be consciously present before him who is truly God, and not before an image of our own creation, just as we seek to make it truly ourselves who are present. When this is made possible, to whatever degree, all forms of prayer can come together. As we rehearse God's ways, our prayers of thanksgiving, praise and wonder are drawn out. As our needs, appetites and desires are laid bare (and this is another reason why our bodies can't be ignored), so our prayers of confession, petition or intercession flow, in accordance with how each part of us appears in the light of God.

We should therefore not worry too much about dividing prayer into sections, or keeping to an order, especially when on our own. Even corporate worship can suffer from being rather too neat and linear. At any point we may find ourselves confessing, interceding or praising. The work is never done, and as long as it is we who are present and it is God whose presence we are in, then more can happen.

In the end, prayer is this one, simple, purposeful act of making ourselves present to God. It does not require that we are articulate or educated. It does not depend on our level of sophistication in theology or expertise in liturgy. In the Church, a diversity of such gifts can serve the body to enable its prayer, but whether or not people are praying does not depend on having those gifts.

For there is nothing that might help our prayer that we are not capable of turning into a hindrance. The essence of prayer may be simple to define, but it is certainly not always easy to practice. Anyone who has seriously tried to pray knows the danger of self-delusion.

I may rightly discover that it is possible to pray at any time and in any place, and it is true that a life of service is a form of prayer even when not consciously praying, but it would be naïve to imagine that it is sufficient to pray just when it occurs to me, or to fail to see that I am avoiding myself by not planning for stillness. On the other hand, I may be so disciplined that my asceticism becomes an end in itself.

I may rightly believe that my emotions may be engaged in prayer, since they are a part of the whole person that I bring to God, but if I seek certain feelings they become their own end. On the other hand, an awareness of this may be so dominant in my mind that I don't realize that my steady composure is the result of the Spirit not being allowed much room for manoeuvre. Similarly, the body is significant for prayer, through posture, gesture, speaking, listening, singing, eating and drinking, and the denial of this is a denial of part of ourselves, but the physical motions alone do not constitute prayer independently of any conscious (or subconscious) intention.

Set forms of words can lull us into thinking that merely to have uttered them is to have prayed, but at the same time we should be careful not to think we are freer for real prayer when we are without them at all. The Lord's Prayer, which Jesus taught his disciples, has been central for most Christians throughout the history of the Church. It immediately takes us to the heart of the life of God in which we share, with the words 'Our Father who art in heaven, hallowed be thy name, thy kingdom come.' By these three phrases we come before God as Father, Son and Holy Spirit: Father, for that is how we address him; Son, for he is God's 'name' by whom God is made known in the world; Holy Spirit, for by him we are drawn to the kingdom where all will be set free from any form of oppressive rule by the Spirit's enabling.[3]

It has often been recognized that these words serve not just as a prayer in themselves, but as a framework which can draw out our own particular prayers, as in this most concise form of words we are placed in God's action.

For various reasons we may at times run out of words in prayer. We may not know what to ask in a difficult situation, or we may have a sense of wonder that cannot be expressed, or we may simply wish to be with God without the burden of finding something to say. Without giving space for such silence we limit what prayer can allow, but with it the scope for distracting thoughts to take over is all the greater. It can therefore help to focus ourselves on a particular phrase from the Lord's Prayer or another prayer, repeating it, not to attract God's attention, but to hold our own. Paul wrote of how the Spirit helps us when we don't know how to pray. We should trust that prayer can happen through us even when we are not consciously directing it.

So prayer is both simple and difficult, as all the gifts which may help us to give ourselves in prayer can so easily become possessions which we grasp. As with our relationships in creation, we are prone to lose sight of the gratuitous existence of the other and regard any encounter as a means to an end. God is reduced to being useful. Prayer is judged by whether it 'works'. We are blind to the irony of exploiting God in seeking the world's freedom.

It is for this reason that all our prayer should be permeated with an acknowledgement of God's glorious freedom, as at the beginning and end of the Lord's Prayer for example. God exists for his own sake, and the life of God as Father, Son and Holy Spirit is about self-giving for the sake of the other. If we miss this when we come to God, then we miss the pointlessness of life itself. We cut away the ground on which any freedom rests. If we have learnt at all to be useless gifts, and to know others as useless gifts, it is only because of God's useless freedom.

We should give ourselves in response to others in this world because they are there, not merely to achieve an end. Similarly, we worship God because he is there. All our wonder, praise and adoration flow for no purpose. We do it because that is our free response to God. We can no more analyze it than we can explain why we should wonder at anything in creation. We worship God, not because he is the ultimate centre of control and purpose, but because he is the ultimate source of freedom and gratuitousness.

However, this is not to pretend that we don't need God, or that our love for him must be wholly disinterested. We depend on God for everything, so we also pray in order that his life may be more fully known in ourselves and in the world. In this sense we do look for prayer to 'work'.

How this can happen has been discussed earlier, where it was explained to be part of God's way of making the world free to make itself. Whenever we honestly pray, we open ourselves and all creation that little bit more to the Spirit, who is able to draw all things nearer to the kingdom of God. We do not know how everything in the world is interrelated, even within ourselves, so we cannot know what our prayers may or may not make possible.

It is important to see that on this view of prayer we are not trying to persuade God, or win his favour by our praise, or stir him into action. God's love is not quickened by our prayer nor measured by the answer. He is passionately active whether or not we pray, but this is a world with its own freedom where God cannot simply effect what he likes. When a disaster happens, for example, it is because the world is such that God was unable to make things otherwise without ceasing to be true to himself.

Prayer is not a lever to move God, for on what fixed point would it rest? Rather, prayer is a lever to move the world, and it rests on God. For the world's freedom, everything is held in place by God through his Word and Spirit as a complex, integral whole in such a way that we are free to make a difference. It is no more or less a source of wonder that the world can be changed by our prayer than by our hands. We may often not see any visible effect directly attributable to our prayers, but the openness to God of both our daily living and our praying has the potential to change the world in ways which we cannot comprehend, and the truer our lives, the more seamless is our praying and our living.

It is through our openness to God and to each other that the world can be moved forwards. This is the heart of the gospel of Christ, and the reason why prayer is necessary for the creation and salvation of the world. When we pray 'thy will be done' we are not simply acknowledging that it is all of God and nothing to do with us. Nor are we thereby conceding that prayer effects merely the alignment of our wills with God's, changing the world only by changing us. We are recognizing that God's freedom to effect his will in any part of the world is integrally bound up with the response made by every other part of the world.

So, to the extent that we can say 'thy will be done' concerning ourselves and the world, we can make a difference. That is why our intercessions need not always be specific requests. We may not always know what to ask. It is sufficient to be with God with our hearts open, bearing up our needs and those of the world. We should remember that Jesus himself in his passion, while praying for the cup of suffering to be removed from him, ultimately said, 'thy will be done'. And the desolation of Jesus in this the most effective of prayers teaches us that the Christian life of prayer can be marked as much by a sense of God's absence as by his presence.

Nothing is constant or certain about prayer except God. Prayer will be as varied as life itself. It may be at different times sublime, laborious or bleak. In this world we should expect nothing else, for prayer is part of the way of the cross, not a relief from it. It is the love of the Lord our God that matters, not the love of every experience of prayer.

17 Christian Living

How does the Christian faith work out practically in our lives? What should Christian people and Christian society look like? How should belief in God the Father, the Son and the Holy Spirit be expressed in what we spend our time doing as we relate to our neighbour and to the wider world?

Everything I have said has been related to the belief that God is love, a love that is about freely giving for the sake of the other without that other ever becoming the end of one's existence. The world is created to share this freedom, and to show God's glory by living God's life.

Yet to say this does not mean that we have a formula which gives instant answers about how to live. That everything is ultimately free and useless, and not a means to an end, may suggest that we cannot *use* anything at all. However, the life of God tells us that everything both exists for its own sake and becomes free in this way only by each being a gift to the other.

Our task is therefore to learn how to receive from the world and give to the world. For example, I believe it is good to use the atmosphere by breathing air in order to stay alive. To each of us oxygen is a gift. But at the same time we face the more difficult challenge of respecting the atmosphere because of its gift to the rest of creation, and for its own sake.

If our relationship with air is not straightforward, how much more difficult is our life with each other. It is little wonder that we naturally wish to make things easier by establishing a set of rules for guidance and reassurance. Even people who break free from traditional codes tend quickly to conform to other patterns. We may smile when we see teenagers wearing their school ties in an identically nonconformist manner, but we all rely on the safety of the acceptable.

As we shall see, rules matter, but first it must be stressed that in the end authentic Christian living is not about obeying a written set of laws. Since Jesus has inaugurated the life of the age to come, the law is to be written within us by the Spirit. God's purpose is that our lives should be motivated from the inside by love from a good heart, not constrained from the outside by duty to a good law. The glory of God can only be fully revealed in a human person, not in a text.

Earlier I described God's life as the music to which creation is called to dance. It is an image which helpfully shows that the following of God's way does not diminish us but allows us to become our true selves. Austin Farrer put it like this:

> . . . the beautiful rhythmic freedom of the dancers . . . What a release and yet at the same time what a control!
>
> What a release and what a control; and the marvel of it is that the release and the control are not two opposite factors balancing one another, they are one and the same thing. That is what releases you, something to dance to; but what is it that controls you? Why, the very same thing; you dance to the music. The control is the release, the music lets you go, the music holds you.[1]

So freedom is not about having the widest choice to do what you like. It does not correspond to a lack of external constraints. Freedom in this sense comes through what we are formed to be. It is about being tuned to respond in harmony with who God is, whatever our circumstances. Jesus was completely free even in his passion. He conformed to the perfect will of his Father God when all around were fearfully calculating how to conform to the expectations of others.[2]

As the Collect for Peace in the Anglican service of Morning Prayer describes it: 'whose service is perfect freedom'.[3] This is the maturity of character towards which we grow. But it is not where we begin, so we should not think ourselves to be such accomplished virtuosos that we are beyond the rules. Only those who have been trained in the rules know when, if ever, it is safe to leave them behind.

The moral principles found in the Bible and taught in the Church represent a distillation of inherited and inspired wisdom, and it is arrogant for a Christian to ignore them. Because rules today seem unattractively authoritarian, many may prefer to think that it is possible to work with just one general principle, such as, 'Do no harm' or 'Do unto others as you would have them do unto you'. These maxims are good and necessary, but they are not sufficient. All you need is love, but 'All you need is love' is not all you need.

It is naïve to think that we have the ability to work out from scratch what is the most loving thing in any situation and put it into effect. It ignores the limitations of our lack of formation. We have already considered how the scope of what we are capable of imagining and performing goes with the measure of freedom which we have so far received. An openness to trust the gathered judgements of others in the community is an important part of our growth. It is necessary and right to question, but in general we are only well placed to understand rules of life, and to bring to them our own contribution of wisdom, when we have learnt to put them into practice.

So rules such as the Ten Commandments have an important place, but they are not without dangers and limits. It is all too easy to regard them as a checklist through which we may justify ourselves. The teaching of Jesus in the Sermon on the Mount challenges our superficial interpretations of the commandments which may leave us complacent.

Furthermore, neither the commandments nor the Bible as a whole give us a blueprint for life. Even in biblical times the law did not yield an answer to every question, acting more as a boundary within which to live. And every generation since has faced issues which were new to their time. The Church must read the Bible in the light of Christ, bringing to bear its accumulated knowledge and experience of the world. This may lead to speaking in a way which goes beyond what is found in Scripture, such as in relation to the rights of women and the abolition of slavery.

If this seems to leave the right way too uncertain, then we should not be surprised given the vision of life as the freedom of a dance rather than the regimentation of a march. We should be wary of any claim to have found a place from which an answer can always be lifted, whether the Bible, the Church, or the rational nature of the world itself, important as all those are to our understanding.

Life is meant to be creative. We are not machines constantly needing to look to the maker for instruction. We are artists who should always be open to God for inspiration. It is through the Word and Spirit that we have been granted any wisdom from the past, and only through the Word and Spirit can we today imagine and express forms of life that reflect God's glory.

We should therefore not think that Christian morality is about striving to discover and live out a fixed pattern of behaviour. Nor is Christian life divided between obligations with which the faith is concerned, and a range of 'free' activity which is of no significance to the faith. The whole is the canvas on which with endless variety we may creatively express the glory of God. The call to gratuitous living neither excludes nor exempts any sphere of life, whether it be family, politics, industry, science, education, sport or the arts.

But the reality is that in many areas of life it can seem impossible to avoid ambiguity and compromise. That is how it must be when the freedom of the part depends so much on the freedom of the whole. The Church is no exception, but nevertheless it should be distinctively marked by seeking to be a community which makes space for the creativity of the Spirit. The Church needs above all to be an environment where people are set free to imagine how things could be different.

The source of this freedom is God, who requires neither that we earn his favour nor fulfil his needs. We must therefore see others as existing for their own sake. And I must know myself to be justified whether or not I am useful or successful. We naturally tend to repress each other by a vicious circle in which we seek to justify ourselves. I cannot be myself because I need to calculate carefully what will be acceptable. To gain acceptance I need to do something to impress and to please. Because I need to stand out in order to be accepted, I have a motive for holding others down by pointing out what is unacceptable about them. And so it goes on.

By contrast, in a free community no one needs to prove anything or hold anything back, for each is a gift to be given and received. That is why both Jesus and Paul speak strongly against judging our sister or brother. If we set ourselves up as the arbiter of who is acceptable, then we not only remove the freedom of others but give up our own. But this is not a pretence that we do not have faults, or a belief that we can all agree to disagree about what is good. Paradoxically this will lead to our faults being more exposed and addressed, because there is nothing to fear. I need to hear the truth about myself from my neighbours, for that is how I may grow. I am free to be myself and to risk getting more things visibly wrong, because I trust I will be forgiven. This is not collectivism – where acceptance only comes with conformity, nor individualism – where freedom needs to be grasped and proved. It is a place where the body sets each person free through the self-giving of each person for the body.

This is the tilled earth from which a thousand flowers can bloom, or the good soil which may produce grain a hundredfold. The Church does not have an ideal model for the whole of Christian living, much less for the life of society in general. But it does believe that where this freedom is laid as a foundation, the Spirit can inspire a community to diverse ways of being gifts to each other and to the world. We need to appreciate the high degree of freedom and responsibility we have been given to create each other and our own lives. It is always tempting to want the security of knowing that we are following the right plan, but God's purpose is that we become right people. God calls us each by name to become his gloriously free children; not infants, who are always within range of the correction or approval of God (much as the Church may sometimes look like that part of society which has not grown up, because it still appears to need an authority to spell out how to live), but adults, who may find God's free life together precisely because we live without God, in that sense.

This has been the vocation of the Church throughout its history, so every generation can draw on old treasures and bring out the new. If the Church bears no heritage then it has ceased to be open to its past. If it bears no freshness then it has ceased to be open to its present. Either way, it cannot be fully free.

So if we survey the Church's life, past and present, in the mix of the glory and the shame we can see where it has been trying to create and express that which will reflect the life of God. Much of this is not unique to the Church, as we may expect, since the Spirit is not the Church's possession, but there are particular emphases which are significant. Worship is an obvious distinctive, at the centre of which is the Eucharist which we will consider further in the next chapter. The service of the Church has been especially focused in the development of health care and education, and in the provision of welfare and relief. The monastic life and the inspiring examples of individual saints are signs to the whole Church and beyond. From the beginning, the Church has sought to fulfil the commission of Jesus by taking the gospel into all the world. And given that it teaches us that we are essentially artists, it is entirely natural that the Christian faith should be the source of such a wealth of fine music, architecture, painting and literature.

Western society has been shaped by Christianity, but as the Church's significance has waned, so people have questioned the point of certain traditions. An example is the Sabbath rest, inherited from Jewish practice and applied by the early Christians to the first day of the week, the day of resurrection. It was fitting that the Lord's day, as it came to be known, should be the time for both the Church's weekly joyful celebration of Easter and for rest. It is because Christ has been raised that we can be set free to be useless. Sunday is a sign that all of our life is gratuitous. In every activity of our lives by which we become gifts to each other, including what we call 'work', we are made what we are, but without our existence being justified by that activity. It is instructive that the climax of the Genesis creation story is not the finishing of creation, nor the creation of humanity, but the seventh day of rest. And the Sabbath principle came to be applied not just to humans, but to the land, which may remind us that the whole creation is made for its own sake, and not merely to be useful.

The observance of the Sabbath principle therefore need not be legalistic. It is both a pointer to God's life and a means by which we appropriate and live that life. The rhythm of the Church's calendar through the year is, similarly, both a way of making the story visible and a means by which it is made the story of our lives. The art of living is about the creation and expression of such effective signs or sacraments, as we look with hope for a time when the whole of life is sacramental. We can therefore understand how insignificant Sunday may appear to people without Christian faith. A utilitarian argument can be made, but it can never be convincing. It is not what convinces Christians.

Marriage is another way of life which our society has found to make less sense as it has become less Christian. The Church can appeal to tradition. It can make a strong case for the usefulness of marriage for the welfare of society, not least for the nurture of children. It can point to the power of the sexual impulse and the potential harmfulness of a lack of any restraint. But after all that is said, someone may still quote examples of casual sex about which it may be asked, with some force, 'Where is the harm? Why deny the pleasure?'

Marriage pre-dates and outreaches the Church, but the earliest Christians recognized the new significance which it may bear. In the tapestry of life, here is a peculiarly inspired motif: a life-long commitment of mutual self-giving, and a love which overflows to others. It is obvious how the sacrificial love of God can be reflected in such a relationship, and in its sexual expression. So no one who acknowledges this meaning can say of any particular instance of sexual intercourse that 'It didn't mean anything'. The Church is called to life which reflects the character of God, and for this reason it attaches sacramental value to sexual relations, the performance of which may therefore be sacrilegious even when pleasurable and without apparent harm.

There are of course many kinds of human relationship which are in different ways holy, or true to who God is. Some marriages are not holy, the continuance of which can be the greater sacrilege. But it is important to realize that marriage is given significance because the Christian calling is to live significantly.[4]

As with the observance of the Sabbath principle, there is a limit to how far wider society may be convinced of this without sharing the same faith. But both these areas illustrate the distinctive creative source of Christian living, and for this reason they have been my focus, not because I am suggesting that they matter most.

The relationship of the Church to society is a whole subject in itself which can only be lightly addressed here. A common misapprehension is to think of the Church only as an institution. But by far the greater part of its engagement with the world is through the ordinary lives of its members, in their families, work, leisure and neighbourhoods. Of course, Christians do not always act as representatives of a particular church, but everything they do, they do as Christians. There is no part of life that their faith cannot touch. This is a most important part of the Church's contribution, though often it is only visible locally, if it is noticeable distinctively as the Church at all.

As indicated earlier, the Church as a body is involved in a wide range of social and educational work at local and national levels, and it also plays its part in the political life of a nation. This last point is often controversial, as many feel that religion and politics should not mix. But we have already noted that the Church's task is to make the tune of God's self-giving love heard, the tune to which it believes all life should be the dance, including its political life. The Church may not have answers, but it has this tune. And if the Church believes that we create true life together by our openness to each other, it will give as much emphasis to allowing other voices to be heard as it does to speaking out for change. Knowing how much we need to grow into life, it will be suspicious of any grand solutions that promise instant prosperity, whether in the direction of totalitarian planning, which denies that the body is only formed by the self-giving of free individuals, or in the direction of libertarian anarchy, which denies that individuals can only be set free by being part of the body. Beyond all our theories and calculations, the Christian faith teaches us that our political life, in common with all our life, needs to be inspired, not constructed, drawn out of us by something beyond ourselves.

This brings us back to where we started in thinking about how we live. For a Christian, the truth that life is about gratuitous self-giving can only be received. Indeed, we cannot make self-giving to be fundamental by our own decision or calculation, for then it is our decision or calculation that is fundamental. If the truth is self-giving, then we have to give ourselves to receive the truth. That is why self-giving is at the root of Christianity in a way that could never be possible in secular humanism. For such a humanist, choice is the foundation of all living.

If it is argued that God must have chosen love to be most important, then it has been forgotten that God is not an isolated individual. Nor is God three self-created sources of love. The Father, the Son and the Holy Spirit each receive the gift of self-giving from the other. God is eternally love through eternally being loved. If it is argued that we could similarly become a community of love, by ourselves and without God, then it is forgotten that God is eternal and never grew in love. We cannot self-start, and the history of salvation is the story of the love of God being formed among us.

It is because life is about self-giving that life is art. Through the Spirit I open myself to the world and my response is drawn out. That is the inspired way we should live. Left to my choice, reason and analysis, I could never find beauty in a sunrise. I have to give myself to find the beauty, in the sense that my calculated will cannot have complete control of my being. Far from science being the discipline that embraces all reality, it falls itself within the realm of art. Anyone who has ever produced any scientific or mathematical insight knows that it is also something that comes to you, which you receive, just like the creative experience in music or writing.

Once self-giving ceases to be the source, the individual will is in control of meaning. Instead of life being an inspired response it becomes a calculated self-expression. Instead of my life being an artistic representation of the truth about the world, it becomes merely a portrayal of me. No one can judge me, but this time not because no one is fit, but because I make the law. I will probably rate happiness as the highest good, so any self-giving is calculated to be just what seems necessary. If happiness can be achieved cheaply and instantly, so much the better.

This is where the road leads if we only believe in ourselves. The kind of culture which it produces is already evident in our society. We should be thankful that the way people live is not always consistent with what they believe, and that applies also to the distorted beliefs which Christians are capable of holding. Precisely because our characters are shaped by each other, behaviour does not instantly change when faith is lost, nor when it is found. God works with secularism where he can; but we may wonder, or rather fear, what a seriously secular society would look like after many generations.

For the Christian, the future is what our patterns of living are meant to signify. The world is art, and we play our part to enable more truth to be represented as we seek to be inspired towards what we cannot yet conceive. We make signs which can both display the kingdom of God and transform us to bring it nearer. It is for this reason that the Eucharist, to which we now turn, is central to Christian worship.

18 The Eucharist

Baptism and the Eucharist would clearly be puzzling to anyone unfamiliar with the story of the Christian faith, but apart from that, someone may still find it rather arbitrary that these two rites matter so much. Why these actions in particular? It is the same kind of thinking which may struggle with the significance of Jesus in particular. God should be available equally to all people at any time, it may be argued. It doesn't seem to be very elegant or fair to rely on such specific ceremony and history. Surely God is not confined or partial, but universally on hand to those who seek him?

We could make the same complaint about the sun. We have to go on holiday to specific places to be sure of finding it. But we know that the sun is constant and unbiased. It is on the earth where the variation lies. Similarly, as I have argued earlier, God has never changed, and never shown favouritism, not even to Israel. The reason why the knowledge of God is not universally even is because this knowledge has grown, and is growing, in a world that is not universally even. To wish for evenness *now* is to wish for the creation of a world with no difference. If we were all clones, all relating to each other in the same way in an unchanging environment, then the heavens may have been endlessly blue from the beginning, but at the price of the earth never becoming anything more than uniformly grey.

If the Eucharist seems odd, then it is because we are odd. And the reason we are odd is that God is odd. It is not just that God is a unity of *three*, but that the Father, the Son and the Holy Spirit are not identical. All the relationships in God are love, but all are expressed differently. We may think that this is inelegant and we may prefer pure symmetry. We may think that it must imply some inequality, and often it has been hard for the Church to believe that there really is no difference in glory within God. But it does seem that the difference which is essential to God is the source of the rich diversity present in the world.

It is indeed a rich diversity, but it would be naïve not to appreciate that this difference in the world is also the source of its conflict and pain. It is perhaps significant that the word 'odd', originating from the idea of the third or upward point of a triangle, also came to carry the sense of being strange or out of place. It is engrained into our thinking that difference may be better smoothed out. Our experience suggests that God's Trinitarian life ought to be angular and awkward.

But the Gospel tells us otherwise. Without any need for accommodation, it was by his self-offering to the Father as Father, and openness to the Spirit as Spirit, that Jesus was able to be the Son, without anything about his life being out of place. Moreover, this is a life into which we and the whole of creation may be drawn to share. As we have seen, salvation is pictured in many ways in the New Testament. One of these is as a reconciliation of what was opposed. When the bank sends me a statement, I compare it with my records. If there is any discrepancy then something must be put right, usually on my side. In the same way, we need to be reconciled by being brought into agreement with God's life. When all that is different in the world becomes able to live in harmony together, without ceasing to be different, then it will reflect God's glory. We will be reconciled to each other and to God.

This is what lies at the heart of the Eucharist. In several places the New Testament speaks of our reconciliation to God being made possible through the 'flesh' and 'blood' of Jesus, and it is this flesh and blood which is set before us in the bread and the wine. Paul says, 'Because there is one bread, we who are many are one body, for we all partake of the one bread' (1 Corinthians 10.17). Here we come together, each in our oddness, and in receiving the gift of Jesus we are made able to become gifts to each other and to God, in what we therefore also call Holy Communion. All the names which are used may be seen to have the sense of gift: at the Lord's Supper we are guests receiving the Lord's gifts; at the Mass (probably from the Latin for 'sent') we become gifts to the world; at the Eucharist we give our thanks.

To understand all this we need to go back to the meal which Jesus shared with his disciples on the night he was betrayed, when he took the bread and the cup saying, 'This is my body, given for you', and, 'This cup, poured out for you, is the new covenant in my blood.' As we saw earlier, the first covenant was ratified by the sacrifice of an animal and the sprinkling of blood on the people. Under this new covenant, the blood is being offered as drink.

We must first be clear that since the covenant or agreement is a sign of God's promise to his people, we should not understand 'old' to imply that God's way had failed or been abandoned. God did not fundamentally change how he relates to the world. The new covenant is the continuance of God's faithfulness.

The Jewish understanding of sacrifice was based on the belief that it was the offering of life which made atonement, not death itself. However, since it was held that the life-force was in the blood, in order to offer the life it was necessary to offer the blood, and it was therefore necessary for the animal to die.[1]

Because of this, the eating of blood by the people was a taboo, for as the means of atonement the blood belonged to God. They could be sprinkled with God's blood as a sign that they were God's people, but no further. So if we think that it is shocking today to hear Jesus say that we should eat his flesh and drink his blood, how much more abhorrent must it have seemed to Jews of his time?

Similarly, in the sacrifice of Christ, it is the offering of his life which makes the difference, not the fact of his death itself. It is the self-giving of Jesus through his life and to the point of death which is sufficient. There is no need to regard it as a death penalty imposed by God. In giving himself wholly to the Father, the order of creation is crucially opened and set free, allowing the Spirit to draw the world towards the future kingdom, and allowing the world to respond.

Israel's prophets had looked for this kingdom, for the new covenant which would give them new hearts inscribed with the law, and for the Spirit to be poured out on all people. The sign that they were God's people would not be an imprint of blood on their flesh but a new life animating their flesh. We can therefore see the logic in Jesus taking the cup of the new covenant, not to sprinkle on his disciples, but to offer it as drink. It is only unthinkable to drink this cup if it is unthinkable for God so to give himself to human beings that we may be infused with his life.

But that is just what has been made possible by Jesus. By our baptism we are united with Christ – an unrepeated action that puts us in a place where his life can be formed in us. And the Eucharist is that means which sums up every other means by which we express and appropriate that life. It is celebrated again and again, for at the supper with his disciples Jesus said, 'Do this in remembrance of me'. How then should we understand what happens when the Church does this now?

At one level it can be said that the bread and wine are symbols which call to mind the sacrifice of Christ. They thereby assure us of our present and future place as God's children under the new covenant. They tell the story and draw out our praise and thanksgiving.

Some Christians do not go beyond this, but the greater part of the Church finds rather more weight in the declaration of Jesus that 'This *is*' his body and blood. Paul speaks of 'sharing in the body of Christ' and 'sharing in the blood of Christ' (1 Corinthians 10.16–17). In John's Gospel (6.51–59), in a passage which is clearly alluding to the Eucharist, we read of the flesh and blood of Jesus as food and drink through which we may abide in him and receive eternal life. Along with the significance drawn out above in comparison with the establishing of the first covenant, it is very difficult to see the actions of Jesus with his disciples, and the actions of the Church now, as little more than a visual aid or an *aide-mémoire*.

In the Church, as the people are gathered, bread and wine are taken and a prayer of thanksgiving is made, which includes the words spoken by Jesus to his disciples. We are taken back to the events of the past, or rather, in this remembrance, the offering of Jesus is made effective in the present. As we have seen, the effectiveness of the offering of Jesus is that we may thereby be enabled to offer ourselves through the Spirit. In this action of the Eucharist, the Spirit is free to work such that the bread and the wine are the means by which we come to share the life of Christ himself. In this representation of his offering to his Father, the way is opened for us to enter into the same movement of self-giving. It is at this point in the liturgy that we therefore pray '*Our* Father'.

All this is to say that the Eucharist is a sacrament, an effective sign. It is a sign of the offering unto death made by Christ which has opened the way for the world to be set free, and it is effective towards setting us free. Because it is a sign, it is not itself the historic offering made by Christ, nor a repetition of it. And the bread and wine remain bread and wine. But because it is effective, it is really the life of Jesus which is made present and received by the believer in the bread and the wine.

Because of the bitter arguments of history over what can be meant by 'really present', it is tempting to say that it doesn't matter. As Elizabeth I put it, 'And what his word doth make it, that I believe and take it.'

However, perhaps unwittingly, that rhyme seems to go quite remarkably to the heart of the issue rather than to avoid it. We find it difficult to believe that words make things what they really are, which is ironic given that it is the Word who makes anything what it really is. We think that the significance we attach to things, what we say about them, is a lesser kind of reality than the material stuff itself. After all, to call myself young doesn't make me young.

But as we saw in the previous chapter, the whole of our living is the art of giving meaning. We are prone to regard culture and our patterns of relationship as an independent layer over material reality, when in fact creation is a whole. All our responsiveness to each other and to other material things is continuous with the responsiveness of elements of matter to the other at whatever level. We are bodies, and no matter how hard we try to imagine otherwise, matter is all we have to enable any communication between us. We give significance and try to make sense of things in the world, and the way our lives develop and the way the world develops depends on the meaning we give. Science is not different, but a part of this. It happens to be that limited way of giving sense which often has the luxury of testing more quickly and precisely the effects of working with that sense.

Most of us do not regard the activity of making sense as a freedom to say what we like. We believe that the significance we give to this or that will make a difference to whether the world will go well or not. The Christian view is that we are seeking to discover patterns of response which reflect God's self-giving and work with the grain of God's way with the world. The Word and Spirit are active towards this end, and our part is to work in tune with this calling and leading. It is impossible to separate our part and God's, for when we create new significance, if it is true to God, then it will open the way for the Spirit to work. On the other hand, where we find the Spirit at work it will look as if we have discovered what God has created. God makes the world to make itself.

Is marriage instituted by God or invented by humans? It is both. Do human beings have the dignity of being unique, irreplaceable, inviolable persons bearing the image of God because we say so? Or because that is how God makes us? It is both, for according to the measure that we learn to regard each other that way, so the Spirit may lead us to know the glorious freedom of the children of God. But a humanity where each regarded the other as a disposable, exploitable resource for their own end would degenerate to chaos and take the rest of the world with it.

As an aside, we may note that the modern ethical issues around the very beginning and end of life come down to what significance we are prepared to give, rather than what may be scientifically true about a particular life form.

So the question concerning the Eucharist is not 'How can bread and wine be anything other than bread and wine?' As if bread and wine were the end to what could be said about it. As if there is a final word that can be said concerning anything. As if the world is static, with a limit to the significance which anything can bear or the art it may inspire. Nor is the question, 'What change must happen in or under this bread and wine that it may be something else?' As if it is always necessary for something to cease to mean what it now means in order to mean anything more.

The question is rather, 'Does it make sense of what is happening to say that the body and blood of Christ are really present in the bread and the wine?' And the answer is that it does. Not because we are free to call these gifts whatever we like, nor because any analysis will find anything other than bread or wine. It makes sense because the words of Jesus have given this sense, and because the Eucharist works with the grain of creation, whereby through the Spirit, by this action of the Church, it is really the life of Jesus of which we partake. By faith we can see this meaning, and our faith is the means by which we receive the gift, not in making it present, but in recognizing its presence.[2]

So the Eucharist is not a magical means whereby we may induce God's blessing through the manipulation of creation. Nor is it an arbitrary incursion into the world by a God who can do what he likes and just happens to have chosen this method to bestow grace. As always in creation, it is what God is able to do because of what the world's response has made possible, in this case the response of Jesus. And at the same time it is what the Church is able to do because of all that God has done through Jesus.

So the Eucharist is not a special act of creation but continuous with everything else which God does. We therefore see here the bigger story, just as we saw that baptism is not merely a symbol of what God can do to save an individual believer, but of what God is doing in drawing the whole creation to freedom from the waters of chaos. In the bread and the wine are represented the ordinary stuff of this world and the work of human hands. By the Holy Spirit they are charged with the self-giving of Christ, and made gifts to us by which we may become gifts to each other and to the world. Set before us in this whole drama is a vision of creation where the giving of each part to the other is the means by which each part becomes a gift. It is a work of art which illustrates how the life of God may become gloriously visible throughout the world. It is a fellowship meal where we share in the good things of the earth, anticipating the Messiah's banquet which the Bible portrays as the consummation of all things. It is done, as Paul said, until the Lord comes, for when all life expresses the self-giving of Christ there will be no need for the oddness of the Eucharistic rite. The heavens will then be endlessly blue at the same time that the world is multifariously coloured.

It is for this reason that Christians speak of the importance of finding Christ in our neighbour. In the light of this hope we cannot see each other in the old way, nor bread and wine, nor any of the matter of creation. This is not a romantic, rose-tinted filtering of all the sin and evil in the world. It is a vision which enables us to see more, not less; to see not just what the world is, but what it may become. Even at its highest, worship is never an attempt to escape the world, as if it is only a shadow of something more real to which we must aspire. It is here where God became incarnate and it is only in creation that his glory can be fully displayed. That is why the true love of God and of our neighbour are never in competition.

Far from making us complacent, as if we have now received all we need, the Eucharist therefore opens us to the gifts which come to us in our neighbours, the Church and the wider world. As I said earlier, it is the means of receiving grace which sums up all other means, for it sums up the whole work of creation. But it does not replace them or make them redundant. On the contrary, because it makes us open to give and receive, it turns us towards them. It drives us to prayer and fellowship, to Scripture and teaching. And because the gift makes us gifts, it sends us out to learn how we may give ourselves in our daily lives.

Where then does all that lead? As we hear the Word, and as we live our lives, we are made conscious of where we fall short, and we are made thankful for all that God has done. So with repentance and praise we are brought back to the Eucharist. Just as we saw how it can never be said that we don't need the Eucharist, so it can never be said that it is all we need. Word and Sacrament flow in and out of each other, and it is as futile to dispute which has priority as it is to argue over the proverbial chicken and egg. When the Eucharist is celebrated it is therefore normally in the context of confession, the reading of the Bible, a sermon, the

Creed, intercessions and praise. All of this draws us to the communion in which our giving and receiving is expressed and strengthened.

More than that, it is entirely appropriate that the context for the celebration of the Eucharist should, in a variety of ways, make visible the gratuitous life which it represents, whether it be through magnificent cathedrals, charming village churches, beautiful liturgical language, sublime music or delightful flowers. Sometimes these things can be despised as unnecessary, but that is largely the point. Their uselessness is a sign of the freedom of creation to which the Eucharist points.

For the same reason it would be nonsense to enslave ourselves by making them obligatory. The heart of the action is simply prayer and the partaking of bread and wine. What matters above all is that we *do this*. Stripped back to the essentials, it doesn't look so odd – more like the everyday life of this world. Adorned with art, it points to heaven. It is the place where earth and heaven meet.

19 Heaven

If the universe continues according to the regularity which science now observes, then the long-term outlook for humanity is bleak. The dead will remain dead. Irrespective of any man-made ecological crisis, after millions of years the earth will be uninhabitable because the sun's temperature is gradually increasing. In the unlikely event that technology had become so advanced that humans were able to discover and colonize a different planet with a more agreeable climate, it would still be necessary to worry about the future development of the universe as a whole. There are various possible scenarios, but none looks good.

Christians hope for something far more, but it is a hope based only on the good news of Jesus Christ. It is not based on a belief that there is a part of us which cannot die. It is not based on a belief that God needs humanity so he must make the project work. It is not based on a belief that God will reward us with an after-life if we have deserved it.

There is no need to add anything to what has been presented so far in order to find reason to trust that the future is not oblivion. The resurrection and ascension of Christ guarantee the future of humanity and the universe. We can know that creation is a work of salvation. We can know that God's purpose is that we come to share in his gratuitous life. We can know that, through Christ, creation has been opened such that God can bring all things to fulfilment through his Word and Spirit.

Today's science is just that – *today's* science. It is a description of how things are. But the whole point of the story of salvation is that the way things are is not how they have to remain. The Church hopes for the resurrection of the dead, when Christ will come again in glory, whose kingdom shall have no end. Since Christ has been raised as the first fruits, all will be made alive through him. It is a hope for creation to be brought to a new freedom where sin and death have been overcome.

For many, this is a very difficult belief. Can it be maintained after nearly 2,000 years of waiting? How does it fit with the argument that God works patiently by his Spirit, respecting the integrity of creation? If God can intervene in this way, why has he not done so already? What does such a belief mean practically? May it not be a disincentive to any effort to improve the present world?

I may have repeated *ad nauseam* that the world which God holds in being is what its history of response has made possible; that God, by his Word and Spirit, is constantly seeking to draw the world forwards to greater freedom; that the openness of human beings to each other and to God is what allows space for something new to spring forth. But I say all this again now, for the principle is based on a belief in God's freedom, and it must therefore apply *ad infinitum*.

There is no reason to think that God will ever work any differently and every reason to trust that he will remain true to who he is. Jesus taught us to pray 'thy kingdom come'. Surely this means that the coming of the kingdom depends on our openness to it. We know that at the Eucharist the early Church used to pray to Jesus using the Aramaic expression, 'Maranatha', meaning 'Lord, come!'[1]

The second epistle of Peter, speaking of the time when the heavens and the earth will be renewed, exhorts the people to lead lives of holiness and godliness by which they are 'waiting for and *hastening* the coming of the day of God' (2 Peter 3.12).

These new things will take place when God makes them happen and when the world allows them to happen. But it is not simply a matter of gradual progress to achieve a critical quantity of prayer or a certain average level of justice and harmony in the world. We cannot comprehend the intricacy of relationships in creation. We would not have known that the time was right for Christ to be born, and we would not have known that the darkness after Good Friday was the moment before the dawn of Easter, and we will certainly not be able to predict when Christ comes again.

The Church is at risk of imbalance in either of two opposite directions on most issues, and this is no exception. If the future resurrection is seen as an intervention, disconnected from God's present work in the world rather than the fulfilment of it, then it is tempting to focus either on the end or on the present, and hard to hold both together. In New Testament times, some Christians were prone to laziness, in anticipation of Christ's return. History is littered with groundless speculation about dates. Political attitudes today, especially in relation to the Middle East, can be distorted by a feverish focus on the apocalyptic. On the other hand, a determination to improve today's world may sometimes be accompanied by a suspicion of any expectation of the miraculous, for fear that it may distract attention from such purpose. 'Thy kingdom come' is reduced to a prayer that our plans may be blessed. The worst thing is to be called escapist, so the hope of being surprised by God is diminished.

But the only way to which we are called is the way of the cross, whereby we find life by losing it. We know the world as gift to us as we become gifts ourselves. It is the outworking of this in our lives which can give hope both for today and for the future. For such openness is what allows the Spirit to work, both in ways which we have already seen and understand, and in new ways which we cannot imagine or anticipate. So we will not make Christ return by standing looking into heaven instead of looking at each other. Nor will we bring the kingdom by only looking to ourselves instead of looking to God. We are not called to sit back and wait, as if it is none of our doing, but neither may we plan the future by our own resources alone. By allowing our attention to be held by today, and the earth where we are, and the people with whom we live, with an openness to God to draw out our response, we at the same time live for the present world and in anticipation of the future glory.

It may be protested that by emphasizing our part in this I am diminishing what Christ has done, thereby making salvation a matter of 'works' not grace. Yet the cross does not take away our responsibility, but makes possible our freedom to respond by the Spirit. And there is nothing that we do through the Spirit which is not God's gracious action as well as our free response. What can be said is that because of Christ the kingdom is sure. We do not know how long it will take, but we may be certain that God will never lose patience, and he will bring all things to fulfilment. Without Christ, creation could never open itself to God to allow him to save it. With Christ, creation can never be so closed to God that it may for ever resist his will to save it.

We repeatedly come back to the fact that creation takes time, for God cannot simply impose a pattern of life. He must allow that life to grow by creation finding itself by the openness of one to the other. We may therefore wonder what will happen at the resurrection if God is to remain true to this way of respecting the world's integrity. Is it possible for a perfect state to be established immediately?

The Church's belief is that at the coming of Christ there will be a judgement of the living and the dead. We should not think of this as punishment, but an intensification of what we can experience in this life when we come to see ourselves as we really are. We should therefore expect that it will not be easy or painless. We should expect it to be something which happens together, between people. There will also be joy, as we see our lives and the lives of others in a truer perspective. It is hard to imagine that this can happen instantaneously, but at the same time it is understandable that many Christians have reservations about the use of the term 'purgatory'. Its past associations with punishment and indulgences, and the common perception of it as a separate place, can be hard to shed. All Christians agree that there will be a purgation; they only differ over how long it will take. As we shall see later, we do not need to consider the life of the world to come as static perfection, so we may understand both judgement and endless growth into the fullness of God's life as seamless and overlapping, a continuation of what can be known now. For reasons already discussed, even here we should not understand God to be seen as a pure and unmediated presence, thereby threatening our freedom. Rather, God is perceived in the glory which gradually becomes more visible as creation is drawn to greater freedom.

But just as in this life we can refuse judgement by closing ourselves to the word which comes from the other, so we may wonder whether it is possible for a person to continue to refuse judgement even after the resurrection. Instead of imagining hell to be a place of punishment for those whose deeds have been especially wicked, or for those who never became Christians, we should think of it as a shrivelling into the loneliness of the self which comes from closing the door to others. While we may hope for all ultimately to be saved, this possibility must stand as a warning if we are to hold that God cannot force himself upon us. If we do not allow the healing of the light of God to judge us, we may bring a rather more fearful judgement on ourselves. As it is often said, the door of hell is locked on the inside.

So far we have considered only the future renewal of the world, but for many the pressing question is what can be said *now* about those who have died. We naturally wish to think of a common environment which connects us with each other. Present time seems to provide this, whereas a future resurrected state seems unreal and distant. So in much popular thinking the resurrection does not feature as prominently as the idea of a loved one living in heaven now, looking down on us. But we must remember that the source of any hope is the resurrection of Christ, to which the Gospels testify. We have no testimony from anyone who has experienced bodiless life after death in heaven.

Even if we take the future resurrection of the dead seriously, it still raises the question of what happens between now and then to those who have died. Many hold that there is an 'intermediate state' of disembodied existence with God in heaven, but there are two difficulties with this. First, following earlier considerations, I do not think that it makes any sense to speak of a human being without a body. Second, if you ask people where they mean by 'with God' or 'in heaven' they are not likely to point you to any physical space in this universe. Yet Einstein has taught us that anything that does not share the space of this universe cannot share its time either. The universe is not 'in' time. The only time we know is that which was created with the universe, as part of it. As the physicist Stephen Hawking put it, to ask what happened before the Big Bang is like asking what lies north of the North Pole. Even Augustine, some 1,500 years before Einstein, understood that our time is created. It does not provide an environment for God.

So we have a choice about this 'intermediate state'. If it is in a heaven which is not part of the universe, then we cannot say that people live there 'between death and resurrection', for that time interval has no meaning as a temporal location for anything outside the universe. If we say that this existence has no spatial location, since it is bodiless, then equally it cannot share our time. If we say it is somehow part of the universe, then we can reasonably question where it is. We can quite literally ask whether we are nearer to heaven in Rome or in Canterbury.

Because time is not an absolute backdrop to reality, we are liberated from having to speak of an intermediate state at all. There will come a time when this order will cease to be. The living and the dead will be brought to live in a new creation with new bodies. It will be a new order, but it will have been made possible by this one. There will not be abandonment or loss of what is good in this world, but restoration and healing in an order which gathers together the whole of the old creation (not just humanity) and opens it to glorious new possibilities. As with other miracles, it will be both surprisingly new and a realization of the potential inherent in the present order.

We may call this a 'new creation', or 'a new heaven and a new earth', or just 'heaven'. It doesn't really matter. But because it will be a radically new universe, we may assume that its time cannot be related to the time of our world, just as it would be nonsense to speak of a physical distance between two universes. An event in the new world cannot be dated 'after resurrection' in the time of our world, and an event in our world cannot be dated 'before resurrection' in the time of the new world. We therefore do not need to speak of an intermediate state because there is no intermediate time, not meaning that there is an interval of zero time, but that there is no time which connects the two worlds at all.

We may therefore suppose that the 'next' that is true of a person after death is the resurrection, the judgement, and the life of the new creation. By 'next' I mean, not next in our time (for there is no 'next' in our time for a person who dies), but next in logic. Logically, the word which makes us now precedes the word which will call us to life in heaven. So while we cannot speak of existence *in relation to our time*, we can speak of *existence*, an existence which is just as real as ours, for it is rooted in God's word.

So we may speak *now* of the saints in heaven, but we cannot speak literally of the saints in heaven *now*, or of the saints in heaven in the future. Time does not provide the connection, only God. And while we cannot sense the departed, or locate them in space or time, the Spirit does unite us with heaven through uniting us with Christ. Heaven cannot be present to us in time, but it is certainly related to us. If this seems puzzling, we must remember that God does not relate to us as God through sharing our time.

A recurring paradox throughout the New Testament is that the new age has both come and not yet come. We have died and been raised with Christ, but we still have to die to what is sinful. Our citizenship is in heaven, and we have been raised up and seated with Christ in the heavenly places, but it seems that we are also very much living on this earth. The kingdom has come, but we pray 'thy kingdom come'. We are saved, but we need to work out our salvation. We have passed from death into life, but when we do not love, we abide in death.[2]

All this seems a puzzle because it suggests that we are two things at once, or in two places at the same time. This did not seem to worry the biblical writers. They did not deny the reality of this world, and of our weak selves, but at the same time they could not deny the conviction that in the death, resurrection and ascension of Jesus, the crucial thing that needed to happen had already happened. The end was already secured. If Christ was ascended, then he was already king, and there was already a kingdom, and if we belonged to him then we were already there. The resurrection appearances and the ascension were not just events in our time, but a sign from the new age breaking into this age.

The heaven I have described is one in which *we* are present as well as the departed. There is no contradiction in this, for we are not on earth and in heaven *at once*, for they do not share the same time. But this heaven is a logical reality even though from our perspective we cannot say it exists 'now'. From God's perspective this heaven is sure, for as night follows day in time, so Christ in heaven follows Christ on earth in the logic of God. That our lives here affect what we are raised to be in heaven, and what judgement we undergo, is still true, without raising any issue of the future affecting the past, or of our present freedom being compromised, for heaven and earth are not related by time. Similarly, God's eternal perspective does not undermine our freedom, for his knowledge of our future is not literally *fore*knowledge, because he does not know it *now* in our time, for he is not contained in our time.

Since the Spirit unites us with the risen and ascended Christ, then the reality of the new age can be known now, in just the way the New Testament describes it. We know ourselves not just as we are in the frailty and struggle of this earth, but as we are in Christ, raised with him. The New Testament speaks of the Spirit as a 'down payment' guaranteeing our future inheritance. So here and now we can grow in our experience of the life and judgement of heaven.

This also sheds light on what the Apostles' Creed calls 'the communion of saints'. It is not clear whether in its original form this referred to the sharing of holy things (the sacraments) or the shared life of holy people. It certainly came later to refer to the common life of all the saints, living and departed. But it is difficult to imagine communion without sharing material things or being material things. What does a communion of disembodied spirits mean? Heaven is rather a communion which, while unimaginably different from what we know, is expressed with new bodies, and new forms of things such as the finest bread and the best wine. And nowhere on this earth can we know ourselves more to be at one with the whole Church, living and departed, than in our partaking of the bread and wine of the Eucharist.

Because of the difficult question of *time* I have trodden carefully in speaking of heaven and the resurrection. We cannot say that the departed saints are now in heaven above without 'now' being as metaphorical as 'above', but there is nothing wrong with metaphorical language. We use it all the time concerning God. So while much of what I have said may seem radical, on the whole it is not intended to say something contradictory to what the Church has traditionally said, but to try to make sense of it. Because the elements of the faith relating to the future do not immediately cohere, questions are inevitably raised, but what I have offered is merely my own attempt to answer them.

20 Suffering and Joy

We are at the end, but how can there possibly be a good end? This is the question which is raised by the toll of the pain and suffering of the world. The Christian faith certainly does not ignore suffering, for to recognize history as a story of salvation is to acknowledge that the way things are is not the way they are meant to be. Indeed, for this reason Christianity is sometimes accused of being too pessimistic because of its emphasis on our need to change. But at the same time, Christianity can be accused of being too optimistic, because it is a faith that God really can heal the world.

Earlier I argued that we are in no position to know whether it is logically possible for God to create a perfect universe from nothing without a process involving pain and suffering. Creation is not God. It is created from nothing, not from God. It is created for its own sake, for its own freedom and integrity. There is no reason for us to believe that whatever God creates from nothing should immediately be perfect.

But having said that, we may still ask whether it is all worth it. Does the end justify the means? And if the means cannot be justified, can there ever be healing in the end, since this question will never go away?

The classic and most intensely focused expression of this challenge is found in Fyodor Dostoevsky's novel *The Brothers Karamazov*. I quote Brian Hebblethwaite's excellent summary of the relevant scene:

> Ivan Karamazov . . . visits his brother Alyosha in the monastery where Alyosha is a novice, and talks to him about his inability to accept God's world, because of the terrible wickedness and suffering it contains. He describes a number of instances of quite gratuitous cruelty and suffering – the mindless lashing of a worn-out horse by a drunken peasant, the pleasure taken by marauding Turks in blowing out a baby's brains in front of its mother, the case

of a child who accidentally injured a Russian general's favourite hound, was stripped and made to run, and had the hounds set on him to tear him to pieces before his mother's eyes. 'I recognise in all humility' says Ivan, 'that I cannot understand why the world is arranged as it is.' He understands that men have been given freedom; but, he asks, is it worthwhile? Is God's purpose worth the tears of one tortured child? Even universal forgiveness and harmony in the future will not make it worth such sufferings. So he hastens to give back his entrance ticket. 'It's not God that I don't accept, Alyosha, only I most respectfully return Him the ticket.' And he clinches the argument by challenging his brother: 'Tell me yourself, I challenge you – answer. Imagine that you are creating a fabric of human destiny with the object of making men happy in the end, giving them peace and rest at last, but that it was essential and inevitable to torture to death only one tiny creature . . . and to found that edifice on its unavenged tears, would you consent to be the architect on those conditions? Tell me, and tell the truth.'

'No I wouldn't consent,' said Alyosha softly . . . [1]

Here we are pulled up and reminded of what we are really saying whenever we try to explain suffering. It is one thing to assert that the world could not be made instantly perfect. But to make that a justification in itself is to reduce *any* pain to the level of arduous training or disagreeable medicine. The horrific depths of human wickedness become merely an incompleteness in the fabric.

The disorder of the chaotic waters is present at the beginning, and this is still evident throughout the world. To say that the world could not be created except by being drawn from such chaos is not to say that we understand it. When Jesus himself was engulfed by it on the cross, all he could say was 'Why?'

For when we think about it we find that in trying to explain the chaos we are, by definition, striving not to see it as chaos. We are attempting to see it as order, as word. It is rather like asking for the light to be turned on so that we may see the darkness more clearly. As Rowan Williams put it, 'All explanation of suffering is an attempt to forget it *as* suffering, and so a quest for untruthfulness.'[2]

On the other hand, a piety which says it is not our place to question God blunts the resistance to evil which is necessary to change the world. We must live between the error of acquiescence, which would stop us asking 'Why?', and the error of denial, which would claim to have an answer.

Because we have no answer, we may do more than return the ticket and reject the possibility of God altogether. Many people do, and suffering is one of the most common objections. But where does that leave us? As soon as we reject God because he allows a world in which a child is tortured, we find that the torture of a child is allowed. Suddenly there is nothing outside of myself to tell me that such torture is wrong. The meaning of the world is set by my decision and taste.

So either way, there is a difficulty, but one is at the shallow end, where there is nothing more to see, and the other is at the deep end, where there must be inaccessible truth. An atheist cannot say, 'One day we may discover why child torture is wrong', or, 'The immorality of child torture is a truth beyond the reach of our cognitive powers of explanation', for it has already been decided that there is nothing deeper than our own choice. The only questions left for the atheist are these: If God could not be justified in setting up the project, can humanity be justified in continuing with it? How is it possible to live with hope in a world which no one could justly have created?

On the other hand, the Christian hope is that God is able to heal the world in a way which we cannot imagine, such that, without any compromise of the truth about suffering, the agonized 'Why?' is no longer necessary. We cannot explain suffering, but we can know that, in Christ, God has taken responsibility for it upon himself. Scepticism about the use of 'mystery' to cover objectionable aspects of faith is understandable, but when all the questions have been honestly faced, to believe at all is to acknowledge a truth that is not our creation and therefore beyond our comprehension.

Christian hope is the Spirit's gift, drawing out our confidence that there is a path between suffering and joy; between sin and forgiveness; between earth and heaven; between the life which we now know and the fullness of God's gratuitous life of which we cannot yet conceive; between Good Friday and Easter.[3]

It is the Easter gospel which makes it possible to anticipate the joy of heaven now, not by denial of the suffering of this world, but by placing the Church at its heart, taking its share of responsibility for the world's salvation.

Of course, we cannot live as if we have left Good Friday behind. We are still being drawn out of the water. We cannot pretend that we have already risen above it all. But at the same time we are now raised with Christ. We are allowed time to rejoice among the mourning. Laughter on Easter Day is permitted, and has been a deliberate practice in some traditions.

Humour is notoriously difficult to analyze, but one significant theory holds that a key ingredient is superiority. This is most healthily expressed when it is a superiority over our former or present selves. It is when we have been able to rise above some difficulty that we may look back and laugh. It is for this reason that the Church's traditional association of laughter with Easter makes perfect sense.

It is easy to see that the story of this world may provide endless material for the humour of heaven, but at the same time it is unthinkable that the reminder of certain evils could ever generate laughter rather than shuddering. Evil can never be considered a light thing, but can its horror ever be surmounted? This is another way of saying that we cannot see how the world may be healed, but Easter is what allows us to live in the hope that we may indeed rise so far.

The alternative is far less thinkable, I find. For it is not only the lack of hope which limits laughter. Another key ingredient in humour is incongruity. But without God, we must ask, incongruous with what?[4]

At the end of that road, nothing is absurd, for all things are permissible. Will the last laugh have happened when the last behaviour has become acceptable? If I decide the meaning, how can I be surprised?

The essence of the life of God in which we share is that we are endlessly surprised. As we are open to each other and the world, we may be seized and held by what comes to us. So in the receiving of the gift we find ourselves to be offered in return. Any temptation to consider the eternity of heaven to be tedious simply reflects our lack of imagination. Is there a limit to the art of life, to the ways in which the God of infinity may be praised through the display of his glory, to the Spirit's capacity to open our eyes to freshness and to draw from us a creative response? We only limit life because there is a limit to what things can be *used* for. But if life is gratuitous, it can never be a job that is done. There are always more ways to be useless, more ways to give and receive, and therefore new heights and depths of what we may become. Because we do not have one, we will never have served our purpose.

Augustine summed it up in his comments on the Psalmist's longing to enter the courts of the Lord:

> We shall not be wearied by the praise of God, nor by His love. If your love should fail, so would your praise; but if love will be everlasting, because the Beauty of God will be uncloying, inexhaustible, fear not that you will lack power ever to praise Him, whom you will have power ever to love.[5]

Notes

Chapter 1

1 Rick Warren, *The Purpose Driven Life*, Zondervan, 2002, pp. 17, 64, 66. Over 30 million copies have been sold and a measure of Rick Warren's influence is that he delivered the invocation at the inauguration of President Barack Obama.
2 Augustine, *Confessions*, 13.ii.
3 Jonathan Sacks, *Morals and Markets: Seventh Annual IEA Hayek Memorial Lecture*, Institute of Economic Affairs, 1999, p. 21.
4 Terry Eagleton, *The Meaning of Life: A Very Short Introduction*, Oxford University Press, 2007, pp. 100f.

Chapter 2

1 It is true that, according to modern physics, the observer and the observed cannot be disentangled at the fundamental level, but my point is that there is no subjective input to such investigation.
2 For a fuller discussion of multiverse theories see Keith Ward, *Why There Almost Certainly Is a God*, Lion, 2008, pp. 67ff.

Chapter 3

1 Augustine, *Confessions*, 10.xxvii.
2 Augustine, *Confessions*, 3.vi.

Chapter 4

1 This 'reflective path towards understanding God as Trinity' is suggested in Rowan Williams, *On Christian Theology*, Blackwell, 2000, p. 74.
2 Rowan Williams, *A Margin of Silence: The Holy Spirit in Russian Orthodox Theology*, Lys Vert, 2008, p. 23.

Chapter 5

1   We are left asking how the devil became evil, with the additional problem that a part of creation must, according to tradition, now be seen as irredeemable.

2   Austin Farrer, *Saving Belief*, Hodder & Stoughton, 1964, p. 51.

3   To put it another way, '. . . we can say that there are some things we can think, say or do that seem to give God that extra "freedom of manoeuvre" in our universe', Rowan Williams, *Tokens of Trust*, Canterbury Press, 2007, p. 45.

Chapter 6

1   Matthew 16.25. See also Matthew 10.39; Mark 8.35; Luke 9.24; 17.33; John 12.25.

Chapter 7

1   Isaiah 42.1–4; 49.1–6; 50.4–6; 52.13—53.12.

2   See Isaiah 6.1; 57.15; John 12.41.

Chapter 8

1   Rowan Williams, in an interview with Richard Dawkins for the Channel 4 television series 'The Genius of Charles Darwin', 2008.

2   For this understanding of the virginal conception I am indebted to Rowan Williams, *Tokens of Trust*, Canterbury Press, 2007, pp. 47ff., pp. 75f.

3   See Luke 1.35; 3.22; Acts 10.38; Hebrews 9.14; Romans 1.4.

4   C. S. Lewis, *Miracles*, Collins, 1947, p. 155.

5   The Doctrine Commission of the Church of England, *The Mystery of Salvation*, Church House Publishing, 1995, p. 12.

6   See Rowan Williams, *Silence and Honey Cakes*, Lion, 2003, pp. 55f.

Chapter 9

1   F. D. E. Schleiermacher, *The Christian Faith*, translation of 2nd edn by H. R. Mackintosh and J. S. Stewart, T&T Clark, 1925, p. 255.

2   Note that, in all this, I am applying Austin Farrer's thought that God 'makes the world make itself', and Rowan Williams' thought that human holiness can give God extra 'freedom of manoeuvre' (see Chapter 5), to the understanding of the whole story of creation and salvation.

Chapter 10

1   For more on this, see Rowan Williams, *Resurrection*, 2nd edn, Darton, Longman & Todd, 2002, pp. 6ff.

2   Colin E. Gunton, *The Actuality of Atonement*, T&T Clark, 1988, p. 165.

Chapter 11

1 Rowan Williams, quoted in Rupert Shortt, *Rowan Williams: An Introduction*, Darton, Longman & Todd, 2003, p. 89 (italics mine).
2 Augustine, *Trinity*, V.9.
3 On this point, see Joseph Cardinal Ratzinger, *Introduction to Christianity*, Ignatius Press, 2000, pp. 178f.
4 From the first Article of Religion in the *Book of Common Prayer* (italics mine).
5 For a detailed discussion of this see Thomas G. Weinandy, *Does God Suffer?*, T&T Clark, 2000, especially pp. 126f.

Chapter 12

1 John D. Zizioulas, *Being as Communion*, SVS Press, 1985, p. 51.
2 Quoted in John Burnaby, *Amor Dei: A Study of the Religion of St Augustine*, Hodder & Stoughton, 1938, p. 221.

Chapter 13

1 Michael Ramsey, *The Gospel and the Catholic Church*, 2nd edn, SPCK, 1956, p. 69.
2 Paraphrased from Karl Barth, *The Faith of the Church*, Collins, 1960, p. 117.

Chapter 15

1 'The slogan of the Church's life is "not without the other"; no I without a you, no I without a we.' Rowan Williams, *Tokens of Trust*, Canterbury Press, 2007, p. 106.
2 More on this from Rowan Williams: 'We have to do what the theologians of the tradition have always done: to take the undoubtedly punctiliar and anthropomorphic language of scripture and piety in talking of God's agency and ask how it can be read in the light of the doctrine of God to which the system of doctrinal and biblical speech overall points. Since there is at the heart of this speech a conviction that God is that on which every particular depends, the one who creates from nothing, the logic of our discourse about God's action must observe the constraints imposed by the implicit prohibition against describing God as an agent among others. And I hope this can be said without inviting the lazy response that this is an imposition of alien metaphysics on the personalist idiom of the Bible.' Rowan Williams, *Wrestling with Angels*, Mike Higton (ed.), SCM, 2007, pp. 269f.
3 'Proverbs seems to say, "These are the rules for life; try them and find that they will work." Job and Ecclesiastes say, "We did, and they don't."' David A. Hubbard, 'The Wisdom Movement and Israel's Covenant Faith', *Tyndale Bulletin*, 1966, 17, p. 6.

Chapter 16

1   From Prayer (1) in George Herbert, *The Complete English Poems*, J. Tobin (ed.), Penguin, 1991, p. 45.
2   From Morning and Evening Prayer in *The Book of Common Prayer*, taken from Psalm 51.15.
3   The roots of this understanding of the Lord's Prayer in early tradition are described in Rowan Williams, *A Margin of Silence: The Holy Spirit in Russian Orthodox Theology*, Lys Vert, 2008, p. 15.

Chapter 17

1   Austin Farrer, *Said or Sung*, The Faith Press, 1960, pp. 185f.
2   As Rowan Williams puts it, '[Jesus] is the language we must learn to be free to speak and act as human beings; even though his "freedom" reaches its fullest point when he is nailed immobile on the cross. There he is most free because he is most truly the compassionate and loving Son of the Father.' Rowan Williams, *Open to Judgement*, Darton, Longman & Todd, 1994, p. 181.
3   From 'Morning Prayer' in the *Book of Common Prayer*.
4   'Our main question about how we lead our sexual lives should be neither "Am I keeping the rules?" nor "Am I being sincere and non-hurtful?" but "How much am I prepared for this to signify?"', Rowan Williams, *Open to Judgement*, Darton, Longman & Todd, 1994, p. 167.

Chapter 18

1   See Leviticus 17.11–14.
2   This understanding has been helped by Rowan Williams, *On Christian Theology*, Blackwell, 2000, pp. 197–208; and Rowan Williams, 2nd edn, *Resurrection*, 2002, Darton, Longman & Todd, pp. 102ff.

Chapter 19

1   *The Didache*, 10. See also 1 Corinthians 16.22; Revelation 22.20.
2   For example: Romans 6.8; Colossians 3.1–3; Romans 8.13; Philippians 3.20; Ephesians 2.6; 1 Corinthians 10.11; Matthew 6.10; Ephesians 2.5; 1 Corinthians 15.2; 1 John 3.14.

Chapter 20

1   Brian Hebblethwaite, *Evil, Suffering and Religion*, Sheldon Press, 1976, p. 5.
2   Rowan Williams, *On Christian Theology*, Blackwell, 2000, p. 155.
3   Rowan Williams, *On Christian Theology*, Blackwell, 2000, p. 154.
4   Based on an observation made by Flannery O'Connor, *Mystery and Manners: Occasional Prose*, Farrar, Straus & Giroux, 1969, pp. 167f.; noted in Rowan Williams, *Grace and Necessity: Reflections on Art and Love*, Morehouse, 2005, p. 131.
5   Augustine, *Expositions on the Psalms*, LXXXIV.8.